# Our Worst Preference
### Reforming the Electoral System

# Our Worst Preference
## Reforming the Electoral System

Brendan Halligan

www.scathanpress.com

Our Worst Preference – Reforming the Electoral System
First Edition, Published by:
Scáthán Press, Dublin, Ireland

www.scathanpress.com

Trade and order inquiries to:
bh@brendanhalligan.com
www.brendanhalligan.com

© Brendan Halligan, 2014

ISBN: 978-0-9927948-0-4

This book is sold subject to the condition that it shall not, by way of trade or otherwise, be lent, resold, hired out, digitally reproduced or otherwise circulated without the publisher's prior consent in any form of binding, cover or digital format other than that in which it is published and without a similar condition being imposed on the subsequent purchaser.

Book design by Cyberscribe.ie

# Contents

| | |
|---|---|
| About the Author | 9 |
| Preface | 11 |
| | |
| Chapter 1: The Urgent Need for Political Reform | 27 |
| Chapter 2: STV - Fit For Purpose? | 47 |
| Chapter 3: Sailing Under False Colours | 79 |
| Chapter 4: A Word to the Wise | 105 |
| Chapter 5: In The Heat of Battle | 123 |
| | |
| References | 135 |

# About the Author

Brendan Halligan became Political Director of the Labour Party in 1967 and was appointed General Secretary a year later, remaining in that position until 1980. He was nominated to the Senate in 1973 by Taoiseach, Liam Cosgrave, won the Dublin South West By-Election in 1976 and was co-opted to the European Parliament in 1983.

He helped create the national Coalition Government 1973-77. He was Director of Elections for the Labour Party in various General, Local and European elections and referenda, including that in 1968 on the electoral system.

He founded the Institute of International and European Affairs (IIEA), and is currently Chairman of the Sustainable Energy Authority of Ireland (SEAI). He is a Member of the Board of Mainstream Renewable Power and was formerly Chairman of Bord na Móna.

An economist, he lectured in the Dublin Institute of Technology and as Adjunct Professor in European Integration at the University of Limerick.

He was Campaign Co-ordinator of "Ireland for Europe" in the Nice II and Lisbon II referenda.

The reform of the political system, and of the electoral system in particular, has been a life-long preoccupation.

Our Worst Preference
Reforming the Electoral System

# Preface

This volume draws together four papers and an article I wrote on the Single Transferable Vote (STV), the first in 1982 and the last some thirty years later. They each reflect a long held belief that the Irish system of Proportional Representation (PR), the Single Transferable Vote, is riddled with defects and is the main cause of a dysfunctional political system which produced two catastrophes in my lifetime, and may yet cause a third.

I first became involved in the intricacies of the Single Transferable Vote shortly after joining the Labour Party Head Office in 1967 as Political Director. On becoming General Secretary the following year I was immediately confronted with a referendum in which Fianna Fáil tried for the second time in a decade to replace STV with the British "first past the post" system of election. Of necessity, I had to become expert in the workings of both systems and learnt a great deal about PR in general and STV in particular from the legendary Enid Lakeman of the British Electoral Reform Society, who came to Ireland to help defend STV and worked with us in the referendum campaign.

In the event, a majority of the electorate saw through Fianna Fáil's attempt at a power grab and, by a thumping majority, rejected their proposal to jettison STV and copper fasten themselves in power. Retribution, however, was not long in coming.

The following year, Kevin Boland, the then Minister for Local Government, carried out a major rearrangement of the constituencies by re-drawing their boundaries and and altering their size. The aim, naturally, was to dilute the proportionality effect of STV, and to secure a higher share of seats in the Dáil than the Fianna Fáil national vote would warrant in a general election.

As a civil engineer, he was highly numerate and far more astute than his manner suggested (the Irish word "glic" would sum him up best). He understood how STV worked and as a party manager, was thoroughly familiar with Fianna Fáil's electoral strength in every District Electoral Division throughout the country. In short, he was ideally equipped to do what he intended to do, and the result was a classic gerrymander.

In the ensuing General Election the Labour Party got a lesson in how STV can be made to work against a party on the receiving end of a constituency carve-up. Despite winning 17% of the national vote Labour won only 12% of the seats in Dáil Éireann and, instead of gaining two or three extra seats actually lost five when compared to the previous election. An analysis of the Boland gerrymander is contained in the Labour Party's 1969 Annual Report.

At the following election in 1973, Labour came to power with Fine Gael after sixteen years in opposition. Still smarting from Boland's gerrymander (and with the two attempts to impose the British electoral system still fresh in the mind) the National Coalition set about undoing what they regarded as a partisan attempt to change the electoral rules of the game. Jimmy Tully, the new Minister for Local Government, was responsible for drafting the legislation, which he did in close collaboration with key ministers, including the Taoiseach, Liam Cosgrave, and both parliamentary parties.

As General Secretary of the Labour Party I was deputed to work with him as an adviser and this gave me a privileged insight into the design of a constituency system intended to ensure that both parties would maximise their ratio of seats to votes.

That meant balancing geography with the inherent mathematical logic of STV, a tricky task. Three seaters, for example, offered the highest potential reward in seats won but carried the highest risk of losses if things went wrong, whereas four seaters minimised risk at the expense of maximising reward because the split between Fine Gael and Labour, on the one side, and Fianna Fáil on the other could be expected to work out at two seats each. Five seaters balanced both risk and reward. If the overall mix could be got right then the outcome would be as intended:

a bonus in seats for the coalition, such as Fianna Fáil had previously ensured for itself.

As things turned out in the subsequent General Election held in 1977, this grand plan boomeranged because both parties lost votes nationally and the preponderance of three seaters in the system leveraged the losses in seats with the result that Fianna Fáil won its biggest Dáil majority ever, twenty-two seats in all. I was a casualty myself, coming fourth in a three seat Dublin constituency.

The period beginning with the referendum in 1968 and culminating with the 1977 election highlighted the first big defect in STV – it need not be proportional at all. It is open to manipulation and, while protected somewhat from that danger because of the Constituencies Commission created after the 1977 election, the protection afforded is only as strong as the law on which it is founded. Legislation can always be amended.

Apart from these high level engagements in the workings of STV, I was also involved as General Secretary in the more mundane task of candidate selection. My experience of this most trying of activities was depressing and exposed the second great defect in STV. As an electoral system it did nothing whatever to facilitate the selection and subsequent election of candidates with the potential to be either good parliamentarians or cabinet ministers, or both. The focus lay elsewhere; the primary requirement of a candidate was to win votes and all other qualities were secondary. From a party perspective, the task of maximising the size of the parliamentary party and simultaneously ensuring that it had the talent to discharge its parliamentary obligations were directly at odds with each other. Sometimes one could get lucky, as the Labour Party did in 1969 when an exceptionally gifted group of deputies was elected, but it was the exception to the rule and their decimation two elections later in 1977 made the point that political talent and popular appeal don't always go hand-in-hand. If anything, the reverse is true. That was, and still is, the second great defect of STV.

The third defect only became obvious with the "normalisation" of politics when civil war passions had cooled and the business of politics had become more mundane in the 1990s. Competition for votes no longer depended on war records but on service to the electorate. As far back as the early 1950s Professor Basil Chubb had identified badgering civil servants on behalf of constituents as a major preoccupation of Dáil deputies and had exposed the "clinic" as a major feature of political life. Academic analysis on the clientelist nature of Irish politics is by now so voluminous that its worst effects can neither be denied nor ignored.

By the time I arrived in the Head Office of the Labour Party in the late sixties the "clinic" was the hub around which constituency life revolved. Assiduous clinic work was lauded by the insiders; neglect was condemned. That is not to say that the intellectual side of politics was ignored. The opposite was true. Policy, however, was the province of the party rank and file whereas constituency work was the preoccupation of deputies, councillors and aspiring candidates. The party had two parallel lives, as it were, and one began to crowd out the other with such effect that a half a century after Basil Chubb's ground-breaking research the "clinic" has won over the "chamber".

This practical experience of STV progressively turned me into a critic of the system and serves as the context for the chapters that follow.

The first consists of a paper I gave to a seminar on electoral reform organised by the *Irish Parliamentary (Former Members) Society* in January 2010. I was asked to consider whether STV was "fit for purpose in a modern democracy" and my conclusion, as will be seen, was an emphatic negative. I did, however, go on to look at other aspects of the political system, such as the method of recruiting and appointing members of the Cabinet, and concluded that they too were unfit for purpose. In short, I said that we needed a root and branch reform of the whole political system if our democracy was to be saved from progressive decay.

To attribute all the ills of the political system to STV would be misplaced, of course, and would only distract attention from the need for other vital reforms, including that of the Civil Service. But, on the other hand, to ignore the centrality of the electoral system is to miss out on how the pieces of the political system fit together and work as a whole.

After all, the electoral system produces the individuals who run the parliamentary system, which in turn determines the governmental system and if ministers are generally below the level required then the fault lies with the process through they are chosen as candidates, elected as deputies and appointed as ministers. It does not lie elsewhere and that was the central thesis advanced to the former members of the Oireachtas (a tough and battle-hardened audience). Without putting words in the mouths of the former parliamentarians, the tenor of the day was strongly in favour of reform.

The second chapter goes back in time to a paper delivered to the Constitutional Club in 1987, where I had been asked to look at the origins and functioning of Proportional Representation in this country and to compare it with other systems of PR in Europe. It drew heavily on research by Michael Holmes, which had been jointly commissioned some years earlier by Bertie Ahern, Ted Nealon and myself with the aim of writing a book together in which we would advocate the replacement of STV with something akin to the German system. Even then there was a substantial body of support among deputies, as there always is, for a change from STV to some proper form of PR. The pity is that the book never saw the light of day; we were all simply too busy doing other, and ultimately less important, things.

The most startling point to emerge from the research by Michael Holmes was that the Single Transferable Vote is not a form of Proportional Representation at all. It was designed and intended for quite another purpose by its author, Thomas Hare. His intention had been to enhance voter choice within the British electoral system and the fact that under certain mathematical conditions it has a proportionality effect is incidental to its main purpose. As the Boland gerrymander proved, those conditions can be easily changed.

The other discovery was that STV had been incorporated into the constitutional order in 1922 without any serious scrutiny by the Committee drawing up the Free State Constitution and with only minimal debate in Dáil Éireann when it subsequently adopted the constitution in its capacity as a constituent assembly. Neither did STV get much examination when Bunreacht na h-Éireann was being debated in the Dáil in 1937.

Thus, on the two occasions when a constitution was being formulated by our national parliament the electoral system was neither the centre of attraction nor even a sideshow.

The reasons for incorporating Proportional Representation into the constitution of the Free State belong, as always, to the particular history of the times.

Griffith had long been an advocate of PR and during the War of Independence had persuaded De Valera to commit Sinn Féin publicly to the use of PR as a means of placating Southern Unionist fears about their political future in an independent Ireland.

In the Treaty negotiations Griffith had felt honour bound to stick to that promise and so STV was incorporated into the Free State constitution with the blessing of the

British government and parliament. The net result was the adoption of an electoral system without any grand debate as to its political or constitutional merits. By an accident of history, Ireland stumbled into a particular electoral system which was not a form of proportional representation at all, as a number of critics actually pointed out at the time. It's hardly any wonder that there have been periodic calls to assess what we inadvertently inherited from our complicated past.

The third chapter incorporates material I had prepared for the Parliamentary Labour Party in 2007 for submission to the Constituency Commission, which was then preparing a redrawing of the constituencies. The submission I had drafted was not used but is included here because it illustrates the singular importance of constituency sizes on the allocation of Dáil seats among the parties, the lesson that had been learned in 1969.

The final chapter consists of an article published in *The Sunday Independent* prior to the first General Election of 1982. While it reflects the concerns of the day it makes the argument for electoral reform in a way that still rings true decades later; a depressing thought for sure. The article looked at the German and Swedish systems as preferred alternatives to STV.

While either would serve us well, my personal preference is for the Swedish model, which I studied at first hand as the guest of the Social Democratic party during their 1968 General Election.

The list system is used in large regional constituencies (such as the city of Stockholm) and in order to ensure a close mathematical correspondence between a party's national vote and seats party representations can be topped up by additional seats drawn from a reserve list.

There is a threshold of 4% of the national vote which has to be exceeded for a party to be eligible to draw on the additional seats, a device to prevent the undue fragmentation of parliament and a common phenomenon in northern Europe.

The concept of a threshold is commonplace with list systems as a means of avoiding the atomisation of the national parliament, such as happens in the Israeli Knesset which, in the absence of a threshold, had no less than twelve parliamentary parties after the 2013 general election. In contrast, the repercentaging of parliamentary representation, which follows the exclusion of those failing to meet the threshold, confers a bonus in terms of additional seats on all the other parties.

Normally speaking, it strengthens the support for the government elected from and by the parliament, thereby adding to political stability. These benefits of the list system remain to be explored in this country, fixated as it is on an eccentric and unique form of election.

As will be seen, the common theme running through the chapters is that the Single Transferable Vote reinforces the clientelist nature of Irish politics, elevates the parochial over the national, enfeebles both the Dáil and the

Government, rewards the worst aspects of political life and penalises the best.

The biggest casualty is the quality of government. That the calibre of ministers had been declining up to the 2011 General Election is beyond dispute. That the decline had reached crisis proportions was no longer in doubt. The events of 2010, with the arrival of the European Central Bank (ECB), the European Commission and the International Monetary Fund (IMF) as our economic guardians and protectors, was proof positive that Irish governments up to that point were no longer equipped for the tasks of managing the economy and protecting society. It was a doleful conclusion, but a true one.

One design flaw which became more prominent during 2010 is the practice of holding by-elections to fill vacancies in the Dáil. This is another relic of the British constitutional principle that members of parliament are the representatives of all the electors in their constituencies, having been directly chosen by them for that purpose. It is entirely logical from this perspective that when a vacancy arises it should be filled immediately by constituents who are otherwise denied parliamentary representation. No such logic applies, however, to a multi-member constituency, yet the British practice has been transported into our constitutional order without any examination of its underlying rationale.

Interestingly, the practice of holding by-elections has not been carried over into either Local Government or the

European Parliament. In the first case, vacancies are filled by the sitting Councillors making a co-option; in the second, any vacancy is automatically filled by a replacement from a list decided in advance by each candidate (or, more accurately, decided for them by the party they seek to represent).

Irish electoral history demonstrates that by-elections generally have a destabilising effect on governments, especially those elected with small majorities. Governments invariably lose a by-election because of the special nature of the contest, which is a lethal combination of local issues and national politics. For governments, squeezed at both ends of this spectrum, it's a no-win situation.

The inevitable effect of a string of by-elections is the erosion of governmental majorities. Deaths and defections within the ranks of its parliamentary supporters can push a government into a minority position even though the electorate had originally endowed it with a "secure" majority in the preceding general election. The events of 2009/2010 were a graphic example of the by-election effect whereby uncertainties over the government's capacity to adopt a budget worked against the national interest in a time of crisis.

The constitutional absurdity of by-elections can be ended by simple legislation; it does not require a referendum. That it has been allowed to fester to the point where it periodically puts a question-mark over the life of a Dáil is yet further proof that nobody has been thinking about the way the political system is supposed to serve the common good.

Governmental majorities can, of course, be lost through defections from their parliamentary parties whereby deputies put their own self interest before that of the nation, the ultimate triumph of localism over the common good.

The Dáil elected in 2011 had hardly settled in than this process began, predominantly within the ranks of the Labour Party. Within eighteen months the percentage of defections had reached an all-time high, a record which pointed up many of the inherent defects in STV, particularly individualism and localism.

These defections were all the more shocking given the perils besetting the state due to the financial and economic catastrophes created by the previous government, not to mention the solemn written pledges the deputies had given prior to becoming candidates to the effect that they would sit, vote and act with the parliamentary party (a formula adopted from Parnell, the creator of the first modern parliamentary party).

These lamentable events confirm that the STV system is open to a fourth systemic defect; the fracturing and weakening of parliamentary parties which is explored in the last chapter consisting of a paper delivered to the McGill Summer School in 2012.

The parliamentary party is the foundation on which parliament itself rests in every democracy and to enfeeble it in any way is to enfeeble the institution. Discipline is essential, not least for effective committee work where the principles and ideology of political parties are supposed to inform the work of the members. Otherwise the assembly and its various organs would become a cacophony of competing sectional, regional and individual interests in which decisions would be reduced to the lowest common denominator to the detriment of the overriding national interest. They may no more perfect than human nature allows, but when used to effect they can be powerful instruments for reform and, in time of crisis, for salvation as the careers of O'Connell, Parnell and the two Cosgraves testify.

Cicero warned that the wellbeing of the people should be the first concern of government. It certainly is their first duty. But if successive governments fail in that duty and if the political system fails persistently to protect society then democracy itself is imperiled.

This realisation may provoke a reaction and create some sort of impetus for reform and the purpose of the following chapters is to help that process by encouraging reflection on the political system as a whole and on the electoral system in particular. They are offered in the belief that conclusions drawn from the evidence can only lead to the conclusion that fundamental reform is necessary for our survival as a sovereign state.

The catastrophe that befell us in 2010 is testimony enough. What we need now is action. As Grattan said, in order to save the country it is absolutely necessary to reform the state.

The general election results of 2011 may, at first sight,

make this conclusion redundant, but I suspect not. Clearly the election marks a watershed in Irish political history, but it is surely just as clear that a new political order has yet to be established and may take a decade or more to bed in.

When it does, the systemic defects of STV will reappear, probably in an even more exaggerated form. Perhaps STV may even prevent a new order from emerging and leave us indefinitely with a political system not fit for purpose in the twenty-first century.

BH

January 2014

Chapter One

# The Urgent Need for Political Reform

*Paper delivered to*
*The MacGill Summer School, July 2012*

# 1. The Urgent Need for Political Reform

## Introduction

There are a number of questions we need to ask ourselves if we are to have a real debate about reforming the electoral system, as the organisers of the Summer School intend. For a start, we could ask how we wound up with the Single Transferrable Vote when twenty-three of the twenty-seven member states of the EU use some form of the list system of PR in parliamentary elections? Why is Malta the only other country in the world to use STV? Why are we an odd man out?

Then we could go on and ask what sort of debate did we have on the merits of the different forms of PR and why did we choose this version above all others? Have we subsequently analysed the effects of STV on the political system and examined it for any systemic defects that might result in our political system being "not fit for purpose", as the organisers suggest? How, in the name of all that is holy, did we wind up in this economic mess with only four former fascist countries to keep us company? It could be said of Greece, Italy, Spain and Portugal that they are to be excused for failing to manage their economies properly since each, after all, is still in the process of building a modern state: in the case of Greece they have only just begun.

But we don't have that sort of excuse to hand. After all, we have been building a state for ninety years, a period uninterrupted by war, revolution or dictatorship. So what makes us different from the other members of the monetary union? Our failure has been spectacular. You could say it has been almost biblical in its proportions. Anglo-Irish Bank, if we need reminding, is one of the biggest banking failures in history, the collapse of our public finances one of the most dramatic ever experienced by a democratic state and the drop in property prices among the steepest on record. The fall in living standards has been one of the most precipitous in modern economic history. The blunt truth is that we are a failed state which is being kept going through the charity of friends. What caused this to happen?

I believe the root cause of the failure is the electoral system. It is being put under the spotlight here at this session of the Summer School under the title of "The Urgent Need to Reform our Electoral System" and rightly so. By way of context, the Summer School brochure makes reference to "public representatives working in an unhealthy political culture of clientelism with an over-concentration on local issues and individual needs at the expense of the common good".

Indeed they do. And I make this prediction: if the electoral system is allowed to go unreformed it will lead inexorably to a crisis in our political system because people will not consent forever to be governed by a state which fails to protect their welfare. That should be self-evident.

## The Social Contract

The social contract between the governing and the governed is based everywhere on the ability of the state to protect its citizens. This is an overriding obligation on the state, which was expressed by Cicero when he said that the first duty and overriding responsibility of the state, or the Supreme Law as he called it, should be the welfare of the people. *Salus populi suprema lex esto.*

When the contract between the governed and the governing is broken then retribution is swift, as we saw in the last election. But were it to be broken again over the next four years by Fine Gael and Labour, the only other combination of democratic political forces on offer, then there is no knowing how the people would react. It can hardly be denied they have been provoked to the limits of endurance and if the various crises facing Irish society are listed - a banking and financial system in ruins, the public finances in melt down, a health system that doesn't work, infrastructure that is grossly inadequate, the spread of organised crime and rampant criminality – then it can hardly be contested that the state is confronting a first order crisis in terms of its legitimacy.

We are facing such a crisis - that is the starting point of this paper. All of the conclusions that outlined here flow from the proposition that the state is in peril because the social contract has been broken. While there are many causes, the poor quality of the public service and regulatory agencies being the most serious, it is inescapable that the failure to honour the social contract originates within the Oireachtas itself. The low calibre of the members, and hence of the Government, were notorious. In specific terms it was the inability of the Dáil to function as an effective legislature that led us to the current crisis.

The electoral system is the root cause of this political failure. It produces the parliamentarians and the parliamentarians produce the government. That neither were up to the primary task of safeguarding the common good is self evident. How then, did we place ourselves in such danger? The answer, surely, is that we have failed to question the political system by which we govern ourselves and have carried on mindlessly with the one we inherited from the British at the foundation of the State. Simply put, we have failed to think about system of governance and this is particularly true of the electoral system.

### The Electoral System

For a start, and to answer the questions posed at the outset as to how we are an outlier with regards to the electoral system, proportional representation was adopted by the infant Irish State partly at the behest of the British, but primarily as a means of assuring southern Unionists that they would be given an appropriate role in an independent Ireland and that their political interests would be protected and respected. Arthur Griffith was a central figure in this process. He had been a founder member of the Electoral

Reform Society, which agitated for the replacement of the "first past the post" electoral system by one based on proportional representation. He persuaded De Valera to make a public commitment to introduce PR when Ireland became independent, a commitment De Valera gave when addressing the 1919 Árd Fheis as President of Sinn Féin. Then on the very same day he signed the Treaty in London, Griffith met representatives of the southern Unionists and repeated that assurance, which he regarded as a matter of honour, and that is how PR became enshrined in the constitution of the Irish Free State.

To be more accurate about it, that is how we adopted the Single Transferable Vote because it was assumed that the Single Transferable Vote and PR were synonymous, which they are not. The reason for the error belongs more to British than to Irish history. The Single Transferable Vote was invented by an Englishman, Thomas Hare, as a means of increasing voter choice in the single member constituencies that are peculiar to the British constitution and for a variety of complicated reasons STV became synonymous with PR. This mistaken belief was shared here in Ireland as much as in Britain, and not least by Griffith.

Yet the difference between the two systems is obvious enough. From the perspective of the elector, Proportional Representation is a choice between political parties whereas the Single Transferrable Vote is a choice between candidates. It is now clear in Britain, as the Royal Commission on Electoral Systems confirmed, that the Single Transferable Vote is not a form of PR at all but is a preferential vote, an insight that has yet to cross the Irish Sea. At the time, many critics here in Ireland, such as James Creed Meredith (also a member of the Electoral Reform Society) and John Commons, pointed out at the time in well written but largely ignored books that STV was not a form of PR but a British electoral system designed to meet the particular requirements of the British constitution regarding parliamentary representation.

Meredith explained in 1913 that, "The system is of English manufacture, having been invented by Mr Hare and supported by John Stuart Mill, and it is largely on this ground that it is preferred in England". This viewpoint had originally been expressed in 1907 by John Commons in his book "Proportional Representation" in which he said "The STV has become the classical form of PR from the great ability with which it was presented by its author, Mr Thomas Hare, and advocated by John Stuart Mill".

But for Griffith, STV was Proportional Representation and none of his colleagues questioned that belief. In fact, they all subscribed to it; hence while Proportional Representation appeared in the Free State Constitution the Dáil took that as meaning STV and put it into the electoral act without any real debate as to its nature or effects. But the Free State constitution at least had the merit of simply referring to Proportional Representation as the electoral system to be employed, leaving it to the Oireachtas to choose by way of legislation which form was to be used. Bunreacht na h-Éireann, on the other hand, is unfortunately more prescriptive in that it refers to the election of members of the Dáil "on the system of proportional representation by means of the single transferable vote". As a result, our electoral system can only be changed by way of referendum, which Fianna Fáil tried to do in 1957 and 1968. On both occasions they endeavoured to re-introduce the straight vote in an attempt to secure themselves in power and consequently there was no real debate in either referendum campaign since both Fine Gael and Labour saw it as an issue of political life or death and didn't engage in the niceties of academic discourse. In 1968 Labour, for example, campaigned on the slogan "The Straight Vote is Crooked", which it is.

That brief résumé answers the question as to how we came to choose STV as our electoral system. It also answers the subsidiary question as to the depth of the debate on alternative voting systems.

In summary, the adoption of STV was an accident of history and since the debate on the merits of different electoral systems was virtually non-existent, we wound up being one of four EU member states not using the List System of PR to elect members of Parliament. Apart from Malta which, as mentioned earlier, uses STV, the other outsiders are UK and France which both use single seat constituencies with MPs elected on the majoritarian principle, a system that in each case has paradoxically become a de facto list system, making Ireland even more exceptional. (Being exceptional is something to be worried about).

## Negative Effects of STV

As to whether systematic analysis of the effects of STV on the political system has been carried out, the answer has to be: not a lot. But one body which has debated the issue is the Irish Parliamentary (Former Members) Association which, interestingly, held a one-day seminar on the "Reform of the Electoral System" on 21 January 2010, the 91st Anniversary of the First Dáil. Here's a summary of what I said on that occasion about the systemic defects of STV and it answers the question of what is required of an electoral system if the political system as an entity is to function optimally.

One of the first requirements is that it should be instrumental in ensuring a functioning, effective, and professional legislature. This is of critical importance because parliament is core to the democratic system as a whole and it follows as a logical consequence that the electoral system must, as a primary requirement, produce parliamentarians who are equal to the task. But because of the growing complexity of political life the job description of the parliamentarian is being expanded to include that of policy originator and public investigator, as well as the basic requirements of legislator and representative of the people. What we find elsewhere in Europe are professional parliamentarians, as distinct from professional politicians, with the time and talent to make parliament work as a national institution. For that to happen, there must be a committee system where the focus is on the affairs of society as a whole; and for that to happen we need parliamentarians with the time and the talent to work the committees.

Does STV lead to the election of such parliamentarians or does it predominantly lead to the return of politicians whose focus is on their own patch and whose primary preoccupation is to get themselves re-elected? The answer is self-evident. The reality is that the election of professional parliamentarians is an accidental by-product of STV because under that system the primary requirement of a good candidate is electability; having the potential to be an effective parliamentarian matters little to the electorate and even less to the party apparatus. It is not a selling point either at a selection conference or at the hustings. So our electoral system suffers from a fundamental design fault and this failure has a negative impact on the supply of talent to the Dáil.

While this is a fundamental flaw it is made even worse by the way STV prevents deputies from doing the work they were elected to do. Instead of devoting themselves to parliamentary duties deputies are subject to the "tyranny of the constant campaign" of trying to get themselves re-elected. This is unavoidable because in a multi-member constituency the competition for votes is continuous and consists of what Professor Basil Chubb famously called badgering civil servants on behalf of constituents.

Badgering civil servants is unavoidable because of the two factors. Firstly, in multi-member constituencies competition for votes mainly takes the form of looking after individual constituents, nowadays by running highly organised "clinics". Secondly, STV is a person centred system and, as a consequence, the link between the deputy and the constituent is direct and personal. By and large, it stands or falls on services rendered by the deputy to the constituent. That concentrates the mind of the deputy.

In summary, the two basic design faults come at a cost and here we can apply a little economic analysis to prove what should be self-evident: STV largely results in the wrong sort of parliamentarian being elected and, even when the right sort is elected, largely results in them doing the wrong sort of work.

Electing the wrong sort of parliamentarian results from what Dan O'Brien in an Irish Times article called "choice architecture", a concept developed by behavioural economists. He argued that the choice architecture of the Irish electoral system means that voters tend to opt for candidates "who deliver for the locality but neglect their duties at the helm of the ship of State". This is an incentive, he said, to vote for those who work only to deliver short-term gains for the locality rather than long-term gains for the nation. He concluded by saying that the choice architecture of many continental systems of proportional representation put better options to the elector. Indeed they do, and they do so through the list system.

The other piece of economic analysis is that of opportunity cost, which, in this case, is expressed in the simple proposition that you cannot do two things at the same time: if parliamentarians are looking after constituents then they not looking after parliament, and not attending their committees. It's well known that in contrast with other parliaments, the Oireachtas has a weak committee system. It is less well known that it came late to the establishment of committees and is still struggling to incorporate them into the way it does its work. STV reinforces this inherited weakness because of the competition for the member's time between the committee room and the constituency clinic, a competition in which the clinic always wins.

## Centrality of Committees

This is tragic because in committee draft legislation can be subjected to detailed scrutiny and amendment but it can neither be scrutinised nor amended unless the parliamentarian has the time and the talent to do both.

Furthermore, it is at this stage in the legislative process that ministers and civil servants are not only most accessible to the parliamentarian but are also most open to cross-examination in public on the purpose and content of the proposed legislation or the effects of policy. Again, if parliamentarians have neither the time nor the talent for this specialist activity then ministers and civil servants will not be held accountable to the extent they should be nor will the political process be as transparent as it could be.

Active committees are central to a functioning parliamentary system but human nature dictates that ministers and civil servants like docile committees; the more preoccupied the parliamentarian is with constituency work, the more docile the parliamentarian within the committee, presuming he or she turns up, and the happier the ministers and civil servants. While the civil service and the government are the winners, accountability is the most obvious loser. But a less obvious consequence is the failure of parliament to perform two other fundamental tasks – that of scrutinising the implementation of policy and of carrying out investigations into issues of public concern.

In an age when people demand to be heard, and take consultation as a right, parliamentary committees can play an indispensable role in linking the parliament with the electorate. It's obvious that if the relationship is to flourish that parliament needs a vibrant committee system and this, in turn, demands parliamentarians who can give it the time and the attention it takes to make the committees work properly. Unfortunately, STV acts as an obstacle to efficient committee work and it is ironic that those who praise it for the direct contact it produces between the deputy and the constituent, mainly as a client, do not condemn it for the lack of contact between the same deputy and the citizen. I have no doubt as to which role should be given priority: the citizen should take precedence over the client.

## The Poor Quality of Government

Another obvious defect of STV is the quality of the government it produces. Given that we adopted the

Westminster parliamentary model of government, in which cabinet members are chosen from the members of the Dáil, then the quality of those elected as parliamentarians under STV determines the quality of those chosen by the Taoiseach to serve as Ministers. This political reality highlights the direct causal relationship between the electoral system and the quality of government. It is purely by accident that we get deputies who are both good vote getters at constituency level and good government ministers at cabinet level. The supply of such dual stars is limited. The supply of good ministers is reduced even further by the exclusion of members of the opposition – usually half the number of deputies- and by the requirement that the geographic spread of ministers should be equitable, a lethal consequence of the localism inherent in STV. Quality and geography are at odds.

It is no wonder that we have poor quality government. Neither is it any wonder that poor quality public service is a direct by-product because on the one hand the parliament fails to act as watchdog and guardian of the public interest and, on the other, the government fails to act as the protector of the public interest and is incapable of demanding the highest possible standards from the public service. The "Peter Principle" is given full rein, with predictable results, and it indisputable that the root cause of this malaise is an electoral system that reinforces the clientelist nature of Irish politics, elevates the parochial over the national, enfeebles both the Dáil and the Government, rewards the worst aspects of political life and penalises the best. The political system suffers and society pays the price. The events of 2010, with the arrival of the ECB, European Commission and IMF as our economic guardians and protectors, was proof positive that Irish governments up to that point were no longer equipped for the tasks of managing the economy and protecting society. It was a doleful conclusion, but a true one. This is not to exonerate other elements of the political system. The restriction of government membership to members of the Dáil (except for a little used constitutional device to include a maximum of two Senators) is clearly an issue for debate.

So too the role and powers of the Senate and Local Authorities, as well as the part played by courts and the judiciary in the constitutional order, and, dare I add, the role of the media in shaping the quality and determining the tone of what passes as public debate. They all play a part in determining the political system as a whole but is a sound principle of organizational reform to look for the core characteristic which sets the culture of an organisation and influences the efficacy of all other units in the system. Another way of making the point is to say that accurate diagnosis is central to proper prescription. In my view, good diagnosis would point to the electoral system as the source of the poison within the political system.

## Political Parties

This is not a universal view. An Irish Times editorial of 18 February 2011, which was devoted to the topic of changing the voting system, defended what it called "PR - STV", the hyphenation being symbolic of the confusion in the Irish mind about the real nature of STV. The editorial accepted that STV required TDs to expend "considerable energy cultivating their constituencies". This was not a bad thing in itself, it said. Voters were given a real sense of connection to, and ownership of, their representatives, it added, while TDs and ministers were given "a real personal knowledge of their constituents lives, making them real representatives of the people". Finally, it deprecated a list system, which it believed would pass the choice of candidates from the voter to the party bosses.

That fairly represents the battle lines of the debate ahead. Since the alternative to STV is some form of a list system and since all list systems are based on political parties it is essential to be clear about their role in society. Political parties are the lifeblood of politics and are the bedrock on which the political system rests. They organise and institutionalise political differences so that public discourse can be conducted in accordance with civilised norms.

By channelling debate within themselves, and between each other, they moderate public feelings and ease political passions. The debates on Northern policy in the early seventies were a graphic example of the value of political parties within the public order. This is also the case with the current crisis, at least in so far as the three main parties are concerned.

But the STV system of election is predicated on the proposition that parties are secondary to the candidate. In fact, the constitution takes this to its logical conclusion by ignoring their existence and failing to recognise them at all.

Now this is a dangerous flight from reality because parties are the foundation upon which the political system rests. Yet our electoral system is based on an alternative reality in which parties don't exist at all. In contrast, twenty-three of the twenty-seven Member States of the EU using the list system of Proportional Representation have grounded their politics in the reality that parties exist. Twenty-five member states, for example, use some form of the list system for the European elections, a graphic confirmation of the centrality of the political party to the political system which is universally accepted in Europe, except Ireland (and Malta).

Experience shows that list systems of whatever variety produce parliaments and provide governments which are up to the task of keeping the social contract.

Our experience over the past decade in particular tells us that STV has failed in this fundamental duty, not because of the moral shortcomings of individual politicians but because history dealt us a bad hand. Nobody chose STV as the best electoral system having carefully evaluated all others. It was bequeathed to us by an accident and it has turned out to be the worst of all possible systems for our country, given the localist and clientelist nature of our politics.

## Conclusion

If these propositions are true then the conclusions to be drawn are chilling, for good government is the central task of society. Yet Barbara Tuchman in her magisterial analysis of history says that what we humans do worst is what we should do best, that is, govern ourselves. She observes that there is an inbuilt tendency within human nature to do the opposite of what intelligence tells us to do. She called this the "March to Folly", the title of her book. She said there were three requirements for any course of action to merit condemnation as folly leading to ruin. First, there must be alternative courses of action on offer. Second, they must be known to those who govern. Third, there must be public warnings about choosing the wrong option.

We in Ireland fulfil all three requirements. By continuing with STV we are marching purposefully towards the political ruin she describes as folly. Alternative electoral systems exist. We know what they are and we hear the public warnings about the defects of STV. Yet we march on.

The forthcoming constitutional convention is an opportunity to halt the onward "March to Folly". I suggest a modern day equivalent of Griffith's Electoral Reform Society be formed. I propose that those who believe the country is imperilled by the electoral system should campaign for the replacement of STV by a real form of Proportional Representation and so undo the legacy bequeathed to us by chance and replace it with a future based on choice. This is a once off opportunity to reverse history.

Chapter Two

STV: Fit for Purpose?

*A paper delivered to a seminar organised by the Irish Parliamentary (Former Members) Society on the "Reform of the Electoral System" which was held in Dublin Castle, 21 January 2010*

## 2. STV: Fit for Purpose?

### Introduction

There is no more appropriate body to conduct a review of the electoral system than those who not only have direct personal experience of the way it works but also enjoy the freedom as former Oireachtas members to assess its strengths and weaknesses with detachment.

That such a review is timely goes without saying and it is appropriate that we should hold it on the 91st Anniversary of the inaugural meeting of the First Dáil. There has been a growing unease about the appropriateness of the Single Transferable Vote as the means of directly electing Dáil Éireann and indirectly shaping the government.

That unease is justified. I have been asked to answer a blunt question. "Is Ireland's electoral system suitable for a modern European democracy?" My answer is equally blunt: our electoral system is decidedly unsuitable for any modern European democracy, and is particularly unsuitable for Ireland. It is failing to provide us either with a functioning parliament or an effective government.

If our electoral system is permitted to continue unreformed on into the 21st century through a combination of indolence, indifference or inaction, then it will undo what was achieved by the first Dáil Éireann in establishing our independence as a nation and will reduce us, once again, to the status of a province.

It was said by Cicero that the primary obligation of the state was to ensure the safety of the people. *Salus populi suprema lex esto*. Things haven't changed in their essentials since his time, even though the 'safety of the people' can be more broadly defined nowadays to include economic as well as physical security. On that score, the contemporary Irish state has failed. The Barbarians are not only at the gates, they have scaled the walls and are ravaging the city.

It will take a generation for us to recover from the banking catastrophe and while the electoral system cannot be held accountable for all that happened it can certainly be indicted as being directly responsible for producing a political system and culture that by any objective standards have proven unequal to the challenges they have faced.

## Three Requirements

A modern European democracy, the subject of this paper, should expect its electoral system to perform at least three basic functions so that the state can fulfil its side of the social contract which binds it to the people.

Firstly, it must ensure a broad proportionality between the popular support secured by each political party and the number of seats won in parliament. This is essential for the legitimacy of state institutions and the general acceptance of their enactments by way of law, regulations and policy decisions.

Secondly, it must provide parliamentarians of the requisite calibre to create a functioning and effective legislature which is capable of framing law, originating policy and overseeing the executive.

Thirdly, it must enable the formation of governments that are representative, stable and effective. For that, they must be composed of high quality ministers who are collectively up to the task of advancing the national interest in the domestic, European and international arenas.

I intend to assess STV against each of these criteria – and in each case it will be found to be deficient. More than that, it will be shown that as an electoral system STV works contrary to the national interest.

I intend to draw on my experiences as a General Secretary, Government Assistant Whip and as former member of the two houses of the Oireachtas and the European Parliament. To add to that background I will also use the Labour party Annual Reports I wrote when General Secretary. In writing on a topic like this there is no substitute for having worked at the coalface, as you have done.

I'm also using a paper I delivered on PR to the Constitution Club in 1987. It contains a lot of research material gathered for an uncompleted project on PR, which I had started with Ted Nealon and Bertie Ahern in the early eighties.

## Proportionality

Let me start with the requirement of proportionality.

The irony of the Single Transferable Vote system of election is that it is not, I repeat not, a form of Proportional Representation at all. It is what it says it is – a single vote that can be transferred from one candidate to another within a single constituency. It is neither a national nor regional form of election but one that is intrinsically local; in our case, one that is mainly county-based. Nor is it a vote for a party but a vote for a person.

On the other hand, all forms of Proportional Representation are based on political parties and provide a direct relationship between their national support in elections and the seats won in parliament. The objective is clear. In contrast, the Single Transferable Vote has no such purpose in mind, although its objective is equally clear. It was primarily designed in 19th century Britain to increase voter choice among the candidates standing for election as the local Member of Parliament. The best analogy for how STV was intended to function is, of course, a by-election or a presidential election in this country.

The system was invented in the 1870s by an Englishman, Thomas Hare, and is essentially the product of mid-Victorian liberalism and of the British constitution, which places the MP, not the party, at the centre of the political system. It became synonymous in the public mind with PR due to the activities of John Stuart Mill and the Proportional Representation Society.

As evidence that it is not a form of PR, however, it is sufficient to quote the Royal Commission on Electoral Systems, which said a century ago that STV owed its peculiar merits and defects to the fact that it was not in its origins a system of PR at all since it subordinated political parties to individual candidates. Of particular note is the fact that it was additionally intended by some to diminish, or even destroy, political parties. Little wonder then that some commentators have called it "personal representation" or "preferential representation".

Only two countries in the world use STV as their electoral system, ourselves and Malta. This alone should encourage us to reflect. Being exceptional is sometimes a cause for concern rather than congratulation. We came to use STV by a series of historical accidents and not by deliberate design. For our purposes, the most important is that Arthur Griffith was a founder member of the Proportional Representation Society of Ireland and bought into the idea that STV was synonymous with PR. He saw Proportional Representation as a means of securing Unionist representation in an Irish Parliament and, as a consequence, so did Sinn Féin. In fact, De Valera, speaking as President of the Party at the 1919 Ard-Fheis, went so far as to commit an Independent Ireland to the use of PR.

On the day the Treaty was actually signed Griffith met senior representatives of the Southern Unionists in London and guaranteed them the use of PR as the electoral system in an independent Ireland. That commitment was honoured and the principle of proportional representation was incorporated into the constitution of the Irish Free State, which, however, left it to the Oireachtas to choose whichever form of PR it wanted to use. When it came to framing the legislation the Dáil automatically assumed STV was synonymous with PR and enacted it into legislation without any real understanding or insight into its workings or implications. The debate on the legislation was perfunctory.

Unfortunately, Bunreacht na h-Éireann went a step further at the behest of De Valera and prescribed that Dáil Éireann should be elected by proportional representation on the Single Transferable Vote. As we know, this requirement can only be altered by amending the Constitution by way of a referendum, something that was twice tried and twice rejected.

It cannot be said that the public debate on either occasion was illuminating due to the adversarial nature of referenda and the fact that the British "first past the post" system was the only alternative being offered to STV. Its defects were so obvious and since it was also called "The Straight Vote" all the Labour Party had to do in 1968 was to campaign against it on the slogan that "The Straight Vote is Crooked". It is, and Labour won.

But in opposing the British system so single-mindedly a great opportunity to examine electoral reform in depth was lost and this has had serious repercussions for it can be taken as a sound rule of thumb that electoral systems have significant political implications for the formation and composition of governments. Different systems will produce different parliamentary results, even with the same distribution of votes between parties.

It is also true, however, that even within the same system the parliamentary outcome can be biased one way or the other by altering, for example, the size and location of constituencies. STV is particularly vulnerable to this form of manipulation. The number and location of the different sizes of constituency have the most serious implications for the size of the parties in Dáil Éireann and can determine who goes into government and who is condemned to opposition. This is no small matter.

Given that the constitution stipulates that Dáil Éireann is to be "elected on the system of proportional representation" it could be assumed that the fundamental requirement in drawing up constituencies should be to protect and give effect to the proportionality of the system as a whole and that this feature would be given precedence over what can only be regarded as secondary characteristics or mechanical concerns, such as county boundaries, continuity in the arrangement of constituencies or regard for significant physical features.

This is not the case at present because the Constituencies Commission in its 2004 report said it did not set out with a preconceived view as to the number and location of the different sizes of constituency but that it tried to suit the constituency size to the population and particular circumstances of each locality. This was a profound mistake on at least three counts. First, it ignored the impact of constituency sizes on the proportionality of the result. Second, it simply re-enforced the localism inherent in the Irish political system, one of its greatest defects, and, third, it accentuated the clientelist nature of Irish politics, the other great defect.

It was the wrong point of departure since there should be a preconceived view as to the number of different sizes of constituency in order to achieve a close approximation between votes cast and seats won. It has always been understood that the size of constituencies is the key variable affecting proportionality and this is particularly the case with STV since the larger the constituency the smaller the quota and the greater the possibility that votes and seats will be proportional.

That being so, it might be expected that the aggregate number of deputies elected in five seat constituencies would predominate and that recourse to three and four seat constituencies would be regarded as a departure from the norm. This is not the case. Indeed, the reverse has been happening. The number of five-seaters fell from 15 to 12 between 1980 and 2003, meaning that the percentage of deputies elected in the five seaters fell from 45% to 36% of the total membership of the Dáil.

The corollary is that the number of three-seaters has risen, from twelve to eighteen.

This development has adversely affected what Cornelius O'Leary called the "index of proportionality" in his great study of Irish elections. Full proportionality between votes and seats is represented by the figure 100 and the index is derived by dividing the percentage of seats won by the percentage of votes won. An index greater than 100 obviously means that a party has won more seats than it was entitled to in terms of the popular vote.

An analysis of the eight general elections between 1982 and 2007 produces some sobering findings. Whereas the index in 1982 was 103, 102 and 99 for Fianna Fáil, Fine Gael and Labour respectively, it had increased substantially in the 1997/2007 period and in the 2007 election stood at 112, 112 and 119 respectively. This means that the three main parties had all won bonus seats, Labour most of all. In the case of Fianna Fáil, however, the bonus was sufficiently large to enable the party to form a government with others of its choice, the bonus being eight seats in toto, with five of them coming from the three-seaters.

It is indisputable that a different configuration of constituencies would have led to different outcomes in terms of Dáil seats and almost certainly to different governments being formed and it is disturbing that the Proportionality Index is not more widely used as an analytical tool to judge the fairness of the manner in which STV is working. If used it would certainly prove the point that STV is not a form of Proportional Representation at all and would remind us that if we genuinely wished to adhere to proportionality as a fundamental constitutional principle then we should jettison STV at once and replace it with some proper form of PR, such as the list system.

These forms of PR are not open to arbitrary choice on the part of a Minister or a Commission but are subject to invariable rules, which give consistent results over time and thereby ensure that electoral equity prevails. I don't believe that we have fully solved the problems evident in the 1969 or 1974 Electoral Acts and I am perturbed at the bias within the system as identified by the Proportionality Index. We have a problem here that will come back to haunt us unless it is addressed.

In summary, STV fails the first requirement of an electoral system suitable for a modern European democracy.

## A Functioning Parliament

The second requirement was that an electoral system should be instrumental in ensuring a functioning, effective and professional legislature. This need has become more acute in modern democracies because the political and economic agendas have become ever more complex both internally and externally. The range of state responsibilities has become more extensive and the economic affairs have become more important than political or diplomatic issues and now dominate the parliamentary agenda.

As a consequence of this greater complexity the job description of the legislator has evolved, with a greater, and growing, emphasis on committee work in which much of the legislator's time is devoted to economic matters. This, in turn, requires a different type of parliamentarian, many of whom are perforce required to become expert in complex policy areas such as taxation, banking, energy, climate change, information technology, the international financial system, European affairs, and so on, if they are to do their work properly.

## The Role of Committees

In short, modern times demand the professionalisation of parliament and the emergence of a class of parliamentarian whose main preoccupation is the work of parliament as an institution, as distinct from providing lobby fodder in blind support of the party leadership. That type of parliamentarian is best provided by a form of list system, which, if used responsibly, can furnish the parliament with a far wider range of talents and expertise than is currently the case.

This, in turn, would particularly facilitate the working of committees, which are the engine room of contemporary parliaments, and the most distinctive feature of the European parliamentary system.

Their most striking feature is the clear-cut distinction between the work of the plenary sessions and that of the committees, as one quickly learns in the European Parliament. The skills required for the committee room are quite different to those that work in the chamber, and not all Irish MEPs have displayed a mastery of both. Dáil Éireann has been shown to be a poor apprenticeship for the European style of politics.

In committee, draft legislation is generally subject to detailed scrutiny and amendment or, at least, it should be, but it can neither be scrutinised nor amended unless the parliamentarian has the time and the talent to do both. Furthermore, it is at this stage in the legislative process that ministers and civil servants are not only most accessible to the parliamentarian but also most open to cross-examination in public on the purpose and content of the proposed legislation. Again, if parliamentarians have neither the time nor the talent for this specialist activity the ministers and civil servants will not be held accountable to the extent they should be, nor will the political process be as transparent as it should.

Human nature dictates that ministers and civil servants like docile committees. The more preoccupied the parliamentarian with constituency work the more docile the parliamentarian within the committee, presuming he or she turns up, and the happier the ministers and civil servants. Ideally, committees should have a complementary role in framing policy especially through receiving evidence and submissions from experts, representative organisations and concerned citizens. In an age when people demand to be heard and take consultation as a right the committees could play an indispensable role in linking the parliament with the electorate.

It's obvious that if the relationship between parliament and the people is to flourish then parliament needs a vibrant committee system and this, in turn, demands parliamentarians who can give it the time and the attention it takes to make the committees work properly.

Unfortunately, the STV system does not allow the committee system to flourish. I think it highly ironic that those who praise it for the direct contact it produces between the deputy and the constituent, mainly as a client, do not condemn it for the lack of contact between the same deputy and the citizen, mainly in the guise of a participant in the democratic process. I have no doubt as to which role should be given priority: the citizen should take precedence over the client.

Finally, committees periodically engage in enquiries for the purpose either of informing the parliament on important matters of state or of informing the public on matters of concern. In some cases committees can be used to hold individuals, organs of the state or other public or private bodies to account when the public good has been impaired. The DIRT enquiry immediately comes to mind as an example of the role parliament can play in exposing malpractices.

But this particular role is rarely put to use for the good reason that it takes time to engage in research, to receive evidence, to attend the public meetings and to sit in private when drafting reports. It is not electorally rewarding, unless the committee hearings attract media attention or the findings make the news. In short, deputies are forced to forego the committee in favour of the clinic. Public life is the poorer for it.

The Oireachtas came late to the committee system. Indeed, it wasn't until the mid seventies that the committee stage of bills was moved out of the chamber and into committee rooms. In fact, there was an absence of committee rooms because they were largely unnecessary. Even now, the relationship between committee work and the Dáil or Senate proceedings is unresolved. Frequently, both take place at the same time and as the power of bi-location has not yet been mastered, even by the most active deputy or senator, one or the other will suffer, usually the committee.

When the Dáil or Senate rises at the end of a term the media will announce that deputies and senators have gone on holidays even when the work of committees continues, often on important legislation or policymaking. The reality is that the media does not itself know how to handle committee work as an integral part of the parliamentary working life and their general level of disinterest does nothing to encourage active committees and reinforces the rush to the clinic.

It is significant that neither the media nor academia have paid much attention to the role of committees in political life. To say that it is not properly valued is an understatement and it is a reflection on our political culture that more is not demanded of the parliament as a national assembly charged with advancing the common good by using committees as investigative tools as in other jurisdictions. Indeed, the obstacles placed by the courts on the investigative role of the Oireachtas as the guardian of citizen interests is only too evident by the practice of refusing to turn up before committees when summoned or, if obeying the summons, of opting to remain mute before the members.

The Oireachtas has, regrettably, failed to address these impediments to playing the role of watchdog and guardian – a failure is due more to a lack of time than to a lack of interest. To my mind, STV has been the root cause of, or failure to develop, a vibrant committee system which would be central to the life of parliament and the public has suffered as a direct consequence.

The list system in contrast fosters the career parliamentarian, a rare enough animal in our circumstances, who accumulates experience over time in a particular field, becomes an acknowledged expert and so adds to the authority of parliament in dealing with both civil servants and government ministers. This is especially important in holding both to account and is crucial in exposing the reasons and reasoning behind the decisions taken by government and the civil service, the latter being all too frequently the real decision makers in our system, often by default, let it be said. In an age where transparency and accountability have become the watchword it is essential that parliament becomes the champion of both. It can't be said that the Oireachtas does either with distinction.

In my opinion, the career parliamentarian is the missing component in our democracy; and it is all attributable to the clientelist nature of STV. This is a serious defect because electorates in modern European democracies are better educated and far more assertive than previously. It is self evident that they are better informed, are less forgiving of stupidity and incompetence and demand ever-higher standards of institutions and those in public office.

## The Decline of Parliamentary Parties

In sum, the relationship between the parliament and the people has changed with greater professionalism and expertise expected of parliament. Unfortunately, the way in which our political system functions has also been changing as a consequence of STV.

The individualist nature of the STV system has become more and more pronounced and candidates have moved centre stage in elections at the expense of parties. Party allegiances and running mates are sometimes reduced in election material, such as posters, to the point of invisibility. Certainly, local and European elections are a spectacular confirmation of the argument that political parties are becoming an endangered species.

The belief that deputies are elected on personal merit rather than party allegiance has major repercussions for the character of political parties in general and parliamentary parties in particular. From my observations, political parties are being transformed into personal claques of individual deputies and candidates. This has a detrimental effect on the politics of ideas and ultimately on the capacity of the state to govern.

As for parliamentary parties, I expect that my experience as a General Secretary was commonplace. The Parliamentary Party was often a flag of convenience for individuals and was difficult to manage as a collectivity when dealing with national issues, which didn't go down well at constituency level. The deputy is at the centre of his or her universe and knows best, that is, about the most important requirement of all, how to get elected. In extremis, a deputy will resign the party whip rather than endanger the local power base; if engaged in a battle with the party leadership an estranged deputy can resign the whip.

This undermines the coherence of parliamentary parties and erodes the authority of the leadership, which invariably is preoccupied with the national and international agendas. In contrast, the nature of politics as experienced by the deputy is primarily local and clientelist and these considerations inevitably take precedence over the broader national agenda. People do not sing off the same hymn sheet.

The direct consequence is that STV produces a permanent tension between the local and the national, between the individual and the collective and between actions as against ideas. It leaves little room for research, reflection or review. This would be bad enough on its own, but the consequences of the individualisation of politics are much wider, as we know.

Incumbent deputies are engaged in a constant battle

to hold onto votes and to win new support but not on the basis of their performance as parliamentarians, or even as Ministers or as Opposition Spokespersons, but rather on the basis of favours done for constituents and local communities.

That in turn has given rise to the tyranny of the "constant campaign" and of the interminable round of clinics which eat up large chunks of time, the opportunity cost of which is less time for parliamentary duties, party responsibilities and, let it be said, less time for family life. The clinic seemed a great idea when it was invented but the sheer grind of running a network of them has forced a number of good people out of politics and ended the career of others, which the system could not afford to lose.

There is no need for academic research to confirm what we already know about clientelism. When I became a deputy thirty-five years ago the older hands suddenly took me seriously. I was no longer a mere Senator or, worse still, a General Secretary. In their kindness they advised me not to serve on any Oireachtas committee – and not to speak too often in the Dáil chamber. Instead, I was to be on the phone pestering civil servants (as Professor Basil Chubb famously put it) or out in the constituency holding clinics.

No greater indictment of STV need be framed. These should not be the priorities of a national parliamentarian. But they are more than that; they are the pre-conditions of survival. And those that don't live by them perish. In my opinion, STV cannot provide parliaments suitable for a modern European democracy. It might have just about adequate for 19th century proto-democracy but not for the demands of 21st century mature democracy.

## Government

This last point brings up the third requirement of the electoral system, namely that it should facilitate the creation of governments adequate to the task of governing in modern Europe. Now this raises two constitutional issues that go beyond the choice of the electoral system. In most European democracies the government is elected by parliament but in some cases Ministers must resign their seats on being appointed to government whereas, in others, non-parliamentarians may become Ministers.

The first procedure is clearly based on the precept that the legislature and executive should be separated and the second on the belief that the task of governing demands specialist skills that go beyond those of vote getting. They both raise issues that need to be addressed because our constitution does not separate the legislature from the executive, in fact, they are intimately linked. Neither does it make provision for bringing outside experts into government, with the exception of bringing in two senators (a device only used twice before and not encouraged by members of the Dáil).

Under our constitution we have adopted the Westminster model whereby the government is elected from and by the Dáil and is responsible to it. The already limited choice of candidates from which the cabinet is to be chosen is further restricted by the fact that half of the deputies are automatically excluded for the simple reason they are in opposition. Of those who are available, the Taoiseach is subject to further constraint because of the need to secure some form of regional balance between Ministers, another negative consequence of STV.

It would seem to most people that the primary requirements of ministers should be political nous and managerial capability but a system which mainly elects deputies for other qualities is not designed in the first instance for producing the sort of government which contemporary society requires and which modern electorates demand. Any co-incidence between the qualities needed for a successful vote-getter and a successful minister is quite fortuitous and this is a systemic weakness in STV. It could prove fatal if the political system were overstressed by economic depression, a public finances crisis, high unemployment and social unrest as a reaction to the state's failure to meet Cicero's law. That danger had increased perceptibly over the first decade of this century.

One solution, arguably, is to hand: the use of the Senate as a means of producing a stream of high-quality Ministers of State. This can be done in two ways. Firstly, the Taoiseach has the right to nominate eleven Senators. They could all be chosen with the national interest in mind. Secondly, the parties have a monopoly over nominations to the Oireachtas sub-panels and can elect anywhere between sixteen and twenty-seven members, a sizable quota of the Senate. They too could be chosen with the nation rather than the party as the primary interest. Furthermore, the parties can influence the outcome of the elections in the Nominating Bodies sub-panels. There is no reason whatever why the Senate could not be transformed instantly into a powerhouse of expertise, experience and capacity - the very qualities which our government system so urgently needs. Not only could such a Senate fill the ranks of the Ministers of State (the Ministers and Secretaries Act permits this) but it could simultaneously supply quality members to Oireachtas Committees (and, indeed, its own Committees along the lines of the French Senate which is renowned for the quality of its reports).

Were this route to be followed, admittedly at the expense of more traditional party stalwarts, it would decisively redress the dearth of talent, which is threatening the political and economic sovereignty of the state.

All democracies are based on a contract between the governed and the governing. When broken the normal response is for the electorate to fire the government at the first opportunity. But if the contract is repeatedly broken due to the continuing failure of successive governments then the state itself will be in crisis. If the various crises facing Irish society are listed - a banking and financial system in ruins, the public finances in melt down, a health system that doesn't work, infrastructure that is grossly inadequate, an inadequate transport system, organised crime and rampant criminality – then it can hardly be contested that the state is confronting a first order crisis in terms of its legitimacy.

We are facing such a crisis. While there are many causes, the poor quality of the public service and regulatory agencies being the most serious, it is inescapable that the low calibre of the membership of the Oireachtas, and hence of the Government, and the failure of the Oireachtas to function as a legislative and deliberative body are at the core of the current crisis.

The electoral system is the root cause. It produces the parliamentarians. The parliamentarians produce the government. That neither is up to the primary task of safeguarding the common good is now self-evident. The argument for fundamental change has been made by the facts. If there ever was a case of *res ipsa loquitor*, then this is it.

## Conclusion

The final observation relates to the status accorded political parties within the electoral system. I believe it inherently dangerous whenever law and reality are divorced, which they are in the Irish political system. Political parties are the lifeblood of politics. They are the bedrock on which the political system rests. They organise and institutionalise political differences so that discourse can be conducted in accordance with civilised norms.

By channelling debate within themselves, and between each other, they moderate public feelings and ease political passions. The debates on Northern policy in the early seventies were a graphic example of the value of political parties within the public order.

But the STV system of election is predicated on the proposition that they are secondary to the candidate. Furthermore, the constitution doesn't recognise them at all. These are dangerous flights from reality. Parties are so much part of the political reality that we take them for granted but the electoral system is based on an alternative reality in which parties don't exist at all.

In contrast, twenty-three of the twenty-seven Member States of the EU use the list system of Proportional Representation, which is based on parties; they have grounded their politics in reality. We have not.

Experience shows that list systems of whatever variety produce parliaments and provide governments which are more up to the tasks set by their electorates than ours. Common sense tells us that our parliament is not up to the task of running the country, not because the moral failings of individual politicians but because history dealt us a bad hand. Nobody chose STV as the best electoral system having carefully evaluated all others. It was bequeathed to us by an accident and it has turned out to be the worst of all possible systems for our country, given the localist and clientelist nature of our politics.

So, the answer to the question, "Is STV fit for purpose?" has to be an unequivocal and emphatic "No!"

Our electoral system is, most definitely, not suitable for a modern European democracy. The pre-occupations of mid-Victorian liberalism are not those of the 21st century Irish electorate. We should join the mainstream of modern European democracies and adopt an electoral system that is attuned to our needs as a society and more in keeping with our national genius; we need one that is based on parties and not on personalities.

After all, it was the Irish who invented the modern political party, both here, in the UK and in the US. It was the open political party as much as the secret armies that won us our freedom. We should put the party to good use again and make it the basis of an electoral system that will furnish us with a functioning parliament and effective government; one that will lift Ireland into the forefront of modern European democracies.

Above all, the Oireachtas should be left to determine which form of PR is to be employed from time to time. For if representative democracy is to true to itself, then it means accepting that the collective intelligence and goodwill of the national parliamentarians are the best and ultimate guarantee of the public good.

There could be no better tribute to those who, in establishing the First Dáil, set us on the path to freedom.

\*

## Electoral Systems in Use in the EU

| | Party Lists (20) |
|---|---|
| 1) | Austria |
| 2) | Belgium |
| 3) | Bulgaria |
| 4) | Cyprus |
| 5) | Czech Republic |
| 6) | Denmark |
| 7) | Estonia |
| 8) | Finland |
| 9) | Greece |
| 10) | Latvia |
| 11) | Lithuania |
| 12) | Luxembourg |
| 13) | Poland |
| 14) | Portugal |
| 15) | Romania |
| 16) | Slovakia |
| 17) | Slovenia |
| 18) | Spain |
| 19) | Sweden |
| 20) | The Netherlands |

| | Single Transferable Vote (2) |
|---|---|
| 1) | Ireland |
| 2) | Malta |

| Mixed Member Majoritarian (2) ||
|---|---|
| 1) | Hungary |
| 2) | Italy |

| Mixed Proportional System (1) ||
|---|---|
| 1) | Germany |

| Plurality-Based Voting (1) ||
|---|---|
| 1) | The United Kingdom |

| Two Round Run-Off (1) ||
|---|---|
| 1) | France |

## Prospective Member States' Electoral Systems

| Party Lists (8) ||
|---|---|
| 1) | Iceland |
| 2) | Norway |
| 3) | Switzerland |
| 4) | Turkey |
| 5) | Croatia |
| 6) | Serbia |
| 7) | Montegro |
| 8) | Albania |

| Separation of Parliament and Executive | |
|---|---|
| Must Ministers Vacate their Seats in Parliament following their Cabinet Appointment? | |
| Austria | No |
| Belgium | Yes |
| Bulgaria | Yes |
| Cyprus | No |
| Czech Rep. | No |
| Denmark | No |
| Estonia | No |
| Finland | No |
| France* | No |
| Germany | Yes |
| Greece | No |
| Hungary | Yes |
| Ireland* | No |
| Italy | No |
| Latvia | No |
| Lithuania | No |
| Luxembourg | No |
| Malta | No |
| Netherlands | Yes |
| Poland | No |
| Portugal | Yes |
| Romania | No |
| Slovakia | No |
| Slovenia | No |
| Spain | No |
| Sweden | Yes |
| U.K. | No |
| * Indicates non-party-list State | |

*Summary: Government and Parliament are separated in 7 Member States; in the other 20 they are joined.*

| Composition of Cabinet | |
|---|---|
| Does the Cabinet have to be composed of Members of the Legislature? | |
| Austria | No |
| Belgium | Yes |
| Bulgaria | Yes |
| Cyprus | No |
| Czech Republic | Yes |
| Denmark | No |
| Estonia | No |
| Finland | No |
| France* | Yes |
| Germany | Yes |
| Greece | Yes |
| Hungary | Yes |
| Ireland* | Yes |
| Italy | No |
| Latvia | Yes |
| Lithuania | Yes |
| Luxembourg | Yes |
| Malta | Yes |
| Netherlands | Yes |
| Poland | Yes |
| Portugal | Yes |
| Romania | Yes |
| Slovakia | Yes |
| Slovenia | No |
| Spain | Yes |
| Sweden | No |
| U.K. | Yes |
| * Indicates non-party-list State | |

*Summary: in 19 Member States the cabinet is drawn from the parliament.*

Chapter Three

# Sailing Under False Colours

*A paper delivered to the Constitution Club
in Buswell's Hotel, Dublin, 1987*

## 3. Sailing Under False Colours

### Background

*The following paper draws heavily on research into the origins of STV conducted by Michael Holmes under commission from Bertie Ahern, Ted Nealon and myself in the early eighties. It had been our ambition, as stated in the introduction, to jointly publish a book advocating the reform of the electoral system by jettisoning STV in favour of a real proportional representation system. The book, unfortunately, was stillborn, but this paper serves as a substitute. Many of the themes were later developed in the paper to the Irish Parliamentary (Former Members) Society and to the MacGill Summer School.*

### Introduction

Like all Gaul, this paper is divided into three parts. The first deals with the origins of the Single Transferable Vote (STV) in Ireland and how it became synonymous with Proportional Representation.

The second outlines the various forms of PR in use throughout Europe and the final section will make some proposals for any future constitutional review.

## The British Connection

The Single Transferable Vote is a British electoral system designed to meet their peculiar constitutional requirements regarding parliamentary representation. An ardent supporter of the introduction of PR into Britain has claimed that, "The STV method of proportional representation is a product essentially of mid Victorian liberalism, whose aim it was to extend the bands of individual choice". [1]

A much-neglected Irish critic of STV, but who was both a proponent of PR and a member of the PR Society, James Creed Meredith, explained in 1913 that, "The system is of English manufacturer, having been invented by Mr. Hare and supported by John Stuart Mill, and it is largely on this ground that it is preferred in England". [2]

This viewpoint had originally been expressed in 1907 by John Commons, in his book, "Proportional Representation" in which he said "The STV has become the classical form of PR from the great ability with which it was presented by its author, Mr Thomas Hare, and advocated by John Stuart Mill". [3]

This emphasis on the advocacy of Mill is an important pointer to the special nature of parliamentary representation in Britain. It springs from the tradition of each constituency choosing a local speaker for itself in the House of Commons[4] whereby the member is theoretically presumed to represent all of its electors and not just the victorious faction. The British system has always been suspicious of party and has regarded the individual legislator as having primary rights over any grouping or fraction. The elector and the elected are presumed to be in direct personal contact without any intervention from outside agencies such as parties.

This theory of representation is grounded in Britain's unique constitutional development and while we may admire the evolution and entrenchment of liberties which the British secured for themselves over the centuries (but not for others) we must not make the mistake of assuming that their experience is universal. It is not. Indeed, the contrary is the case, a point that will become more evident as this paper progresses.

Representation in the British system is based directly on electors and the member represents the whole constituency, not a faction. The Royal Commission on Electoral Systems commended the STV system because it secured "the return of men as men, not as party units, a purpose which it is well calculated to serve."[5] Ernest Naville considered STV a British form of PR because it was "a system which leaves the electors face to face with the candidates without the intervention of lists nominated by parties"[6] and John J. Humphreys in his book on Proportional Representation published in 1911 similarly commended STV because it based "representation upon electors and preserves to them freedom to vote as they pleased".[7]

The Electoral Reform Society in presenting its case in 1982 for the introduction of STV into the UK argued that, "the most important among its attributes is its effectiveness in giving the individual his say in the British system of Government".[8] This is an attribute which may come as a shock to the Irish supporters of STV but this Englishness of the system has long been recognized within that country as its most prominent feature.

The system was simultaneously, but separately, invented by Thomas Hare and Carl Andrae of Denmark in the 1850s and, indeed, Andrae's system was briefly used in the Danish upper house before being discarded. It has never been used elsewhere on the continent where the choice of electoral system invariably came down in favour of the list form of Proportional Representation and which was introduced by twelve countries over a twenty year period 1899-1920 in the following chronological order: Belgium (1899), Finland (1906), which interestingly was then enjoying a form of Home Rule within the Russian Empire, Sweden (1909), Portugal and Bulgaria (1911), Switzerland (1918), Germany, Italy, Austria and Holland (1919), and Norway and Denmark (1920).[9]

The reason why these twelve countries chose a list form of PR is that, coming relatively late to representative democracy, they already had well organized political parties when their democratic parliaments were established. Parties seemed the natural and logical foundation for the electoral system rather than the individual elector.

This is of profound significance for any future consideration of electoral systems in Ireland because we have incorporated, without any fundamental analysis, a system which, as the Royal Commission noted, "owes its peculiar merits and defects to the fact that, subordinating as it does the party to the person, is not in its origins a system of PR at all". The Commission went on to describe STV as more a system of "personal representation" or as other authors have called it "preferential representation".[10] Meredith had identified this defining characteristic of the system when he observed that, "the warmest advocates of STV will generally be found to be those who look with strong disfavour on the system of party government".[11] John Commons had gone further when he alleged that, "the Hare system is advocated by those who, in a too doctrinaire fashion, wish to abolish political parties".

In concluding this analysis as to the reasons why the British rejected any form of the list system it is sufficient to restate that "in England, representation has never theoretically been based upon party"[12] and that for them the cardinal defect of the list system is that it would "completely break the link between the M.P. and his/her constituents"[13] and place real power in the hands of party leaders.[14] The truly damning British indictment is that "no list system takes the final selection of candidates entirely out of the hands of the party managers and puts it where it belongs, in the hands of the voters themselves".[15]

Even list systems that allow for the expression of preferences among candidates have been rejected. For example, the Royal Commission dismissed the Belgian system because it "emphasizes and stereotypes party divisions in a way which is incompatible with the more elastic ideas of British politics". The stereotyping of British parties and the rigid party division which have characterized UK politics since the collapse of the Liberals in the 1920s are the most persuasive proof that ideology is not science and that life itself is the ultimate debunker of even the most pretentious propagandists.

Yet, notwithstanding all experience to the contrary, the two main beneficiaries of the English system are determined to stand out against the list system of PR even to the extent of blocking the introduction of a common electoral system for direct elections to the European Parliament in 1979. Ten of the then twelve member states chose the list system for the European elections, some on a national basis, like France and Germany, with others using regions, like Belgium and Italy. Some allow preferential voting for candidates, like Denmark, while others preclude any alteration to the list. But whatever the variations the fact remains that they are fundamentally using an electoral system based on party rather than individual representation.

Ireland is one of the two exceptions to this otherwise universal rule, an eccentricity that will grow more embarrassing as the Community moves towards greater harmonization of the system used for electing MEPs. The reason is that we were foisted with a British electoral system and the intellectual leap to a continental system has so far proven to be beyond our intellectual capacities. If Keynes could remark that statesmen were too often the prisoners of long defunct economists how much more true is it that we Irish are the prisoners of long defunct constitutional arguments about electoral systems in Britain. The story as to how we came by STV is too little known and can do with plenty of airing, particularly in the context of a constitutional review.

## Adopted by Default

The Single Transferrable Vote was adopted as our electoral system by default. There were two reasons why it was imposed on the nascent Irish Free State. The first was the political imperative of securing fair representation for minorities, such as the Southern Unionists. That was the general reason. The specific reason was that having decided on PR the only version considered was that which appealed to the English cast of mind, viz STV.

The idea that a form of PR be adopted for Ireland was first suggested to the British Government by the Proportional Representation Society in 1911 as a way out of the impasse created by the Unionist opposition to the Irish Home Rule Bill.[16]

It was also a way of popularizing the STV within Britain which, one suspects, was the real reason for proposing it for Ireland. An amendment to have all elections to the House of Commons carried out under PR was defeated but others were carried which would have introduced PR for constituencies returning three or more candidates to the House of Commons and for all elections to the senate.[17]

At that time, the fundamental political issue for the

British Government was the conflict of interests between the Nationalist and Unionist communities with the resolution of these competing interests the primary preoccupation of British policy makers for the next decade. For this reason, Asquith, the Prime Minister, actually approved of the introduction of PR at some date in order to protect the minority although he interestingly refused to specify the particular form of PR to be adopted, remarking loftily that "I do not commit myself to the minute details".[18]

The Proportional Representational Society, however, mounted an intense lobby through direct approaches to all MPs and "approached the leaders on both sides with a view to securing their support"[19] with the result that "the government adopted the Amendment of the Proportional Representation Society".[20] Proposing the adoption of STV for the Senate, the debate on the amendment dealt exclusively with the pros and cons of proportional systems against majority systems and no distinction between various forms of PR appears to have been made.

It was only in the later debate on introducing STV for the Irish House of Commons that any appreciation between the various PR systems was shown. Sir J.D. Rees argued that STV was more suited to Ireland because it gave the independents a better chance of election, a prophecy which has, alas, proven too true.[21] Sir A. Mond opposed list systems on the grounds that they were based on parties,[22] thus emphasizing once again the British antipathy to parliamentary parties except as a casual arrangement between independently elected members.

The whole thrust of the debate, however, was to equate proportional representation with the single transferable vote, an equation which was to have repercussions down to the present day.

The next episode in the saga occurred five years later when the Royal Commission on Electoral Systems recommended the adoption of STV in Britain partially due to the submission it received from the PR Society.[23] The recommendation was rejected but, as Enid Lakeman has noted, the seven years spent working on the report put the idea of STV into the minds of MPs.[24]

The breakthrough came a year later when STV was introduced for the borough Council elections in Sligo, the first time that it was used in Ireland. It was introduced quite blatantly "as a device to protect minority opinion".[25]

But the reaction by all sides to the use of STV was favourable. The Sligo Champion said the system had justified its adoption on the grounds that "It is as easy as the old way; it is a big improvement, and it is absolutely fair." The Unionist Sligo Independent trumpeted, "Sligo has the honour of being the first municipality in Ireland to adopt the principle, and everybody agrees it was a great success".

In the following year a bill was introduced to provide for Proportional Representation in all local elections in Ireland and during the debate the Attorney General for Ireland (A.W. Samuels K.C.) frankly admitted that, "the Government hoped to blunt the edge of Sinn Féin success in the three Southern provinces, and likewise to secure Nationalist representation in Ulster".[26] The elections were held in January 1920 and as part of its policy of trying to engineer adequate minority representation, the Government made no funds available to educate voters in the intricacies of the new system but Sinn Féin conducted its own campaign sufficiently well to ensure success.[27]

About this time the Sinn Féin leaders, Arthur Griffith and Eamon De Valera, declared an adherence to the principle of PR from which they never departed. At the Sinn Féin Ard Fheis in July 1919 De Valera, speaking as President of the party, said "Minorities have rights, and if Sinn Féin have all the machinery of government in their power, they would secure the rights of minorities. Every man living in this Ireland is of equal value in it, and every man and woman would get the share to which he or she is entitled. Whether PR benefited us or not, I would be in favour of the principle, because it is justice".

By this time the momentum in favour of using PR in Ireland was unstoppable but so too was the equation between PR and the STV arising from British prejudice against the list system and Irish ignorance of alternate forms of PR. Thus, when the Government of Ireland Bills were debated in the British House of Commons STV became the chosen electoral system virtually without a contest. The subsequent elections in May 1921 to the two Irish Houses of Commons were held under STV, although the members of the Southern House were returned unopposed.

When it came, therefore, to devising an electoral system for the Irish Free State the situation was one of *fait accompli*. As has been mentioned, Arthur Griffith, who had been a founding member of the PR Society of Ireland, was one of the system's leading advocates, with the equation again being made that the STV was PR in toto. Griffith promised the adoption of PR in order to secure representation for Southern Unionists[28] and the indications are that the guarantee was accepted without question.

More than that, Griffith's word seems to have been so binding that, as far as research can discover so far, the Constitutional Committee set up to draft the Free State Constitution appears not to have discussed the electoral system at all. In his essay on *The Drafting of the Irish Free State Constitution*, Brian Farrell[29] simply states that "all approved" of the PR electoral system. It was probably outside the frame of reference for the Committee, a conclusion arrived at by analogy since the issue of a Second Chamber was immediately pulled out of discussion on the grounds that Griffith had assured Southern Unionists that there would be an upper house.[30] Presumably, therefore, the adoption of PR was taken as a *sine qua non* for the new constitution.

It is, nonetheless, noteworthy that the Free State Constitution did not prescribe STV as the electoral system to be used but simply stated that TDs be elected according to the principle of PR, leaving the details of the electoral system to ordinary law.[31] This sophistication of approach and its manifest confidence in the good sense of the legislature contrasts starkly with the pedantic exactness of the 1937 Constitution. That sophistication was, however, not yet present when the Fourth Dáil came to discuss the legislation establishing the electoral system. Deputies showed no comprehension of any form of PR other than STV and their "speeches revealed a complete ignorance of the list systems".[32]

It was plain, records Cornelius O'Leary,[33] that the constitutional directive, "The Principles of Proportional Representation," was going to be interpreted to mean the single transferrable vote, the only form of PR of which the Irish had any experience".

It is not unfair to conclude that STV came to Ireland by a combination of chance occurrences, ignorance of alternative methods of election, indifference by Irish leaders as to the mechanics of electoral systems and their collective lack of comprehension of the competing principles of parliamentary representation as expressed in England and the Continent.

As a result, Ireland found itself with a system of election originally intended for a country with a totally different parliamentary tradition and constitution. It is a major irony of history that in securing our national independence we finished up passively accepting without examination "the only peculiarly British brand of PR".[34]

"Need this peculiarity of the English mind count for much in Ireland?" asked Meredith in 1913.[35] Unfortunately it has. And it still does.

## Voting Systems in Europe

Within the European Community eight of the twelve Member States use the list system of Proportional Representation in some form or another. The three Scandinavian countries outside the Community all use a variation of the list system, as do Austria and Switzerland. So, of the seventeen democracies in Western Europe, thirteen use the list system of PR.[36]

## Germany

Of the exceptions to the classic form of list PR perhaps Germany is the most interesting. The German electoral system is a unique combination of the British 'first-past-the-post' method of election, which applies to one half of the Bundestag, and a conventional list system, which applies to the other half. The ultimate objective of the system is to give each party a percentage share of the Bundestag seats equivalent to its national vote, provided the party receives more than 5% of the national vote.

In essence, the German system is a combination of single member constituencies with simple majority voting, as in the UK, plus multimember constituencies with PR. This has often been called the 'additional vote' system because the individual voter has two separate votes to cast. The first is for a candidate in a single member constituency just as in a British election. But the second is for a party list presented within a Land and it is the percentage of these votes over the whole country, which determines the overall number of seats to be won by a party in the Bundestag.

So, the overall system works out simply enough. The votes for the party list determine the total number of seats in parliament. The seats won in the constituencies are aggregated and subtracted from this number and the balance is drawn from the list. If a party wins more seats in the constituencies than it is entitled to by its nation-wide proportion then it is permitted to keep the surplus.

As mentioned, a party must gain either 5% of the total vote in the whole country or three of the constituency seats. It is possible for a party to win no seats whatever in the single member constituencies and yet be awarded seats in the Bundestag if its national vote on the list system exceeds 5%. This, in fact, is what has generally happened with the Liberal Party, the FDP, which is the party around which German Governments now pivot. Without them the German political system would have degenerated into a straightforward two party system. But without the electoral system, there would be no Liberals.

It is salutary to remember that the FDP has seldom won seats in a single member constituency yet it constantly provides key Governmental Ministers, such as Foreign Minister Genscher in a coalition of the Centre Left with the SPD or of the Centre Right with the CDU/CSU. The Liberals literally make or break Governments, as they demonstrated when they walked out of Helmut Schmidt's coalition and took up instead with Kohl who has been Chancellor ever since. An electoral system conferring much power in a tiny faction would be denounced out of hand in Ireland and dismissed as undemocratic. It would be condemned with even greater vehemence in the UK but it is ironic to recall that it was within the British occupied zone of Germany that a combination of the Weimar Republic list system and the first-past-the-post system was first used in the local elections of 1945 and then used on a country wide basis.[37]

The way in which German elections normally work out is that the Christian Democrats win about two thirds of the constituency seats, the Social Democrats the remaining one third, with no seats at all for either the Liberals or the Greens. In fact the Greens have not won in a constituency as yet and all their members come from the list.

The combination of the two systems leads to highly intelligent tactical voting by the various party supporters. For example, conservative voters often give their first vote to the Liberals in order to ensure their coalition partners' presence in the Bundestag. Likewise, Green supporters often vote SPD on the first ballot since they know it would otherwise be a wasted vote. The sophistication of voting refutes any criticisms of the system on the ground that it is inflexible. On the contrary, it is subtly flexible.

Because of its proportionality effect and the actual use of a Party list, it is permissible to include Germany amongst the countries using the list system. That would raise the number to nine of the twelve European Community Member States using the list system.

## France

Contrary to popular belief, France has never at any time elected her parliament by proportional system except in 1945, 1946 and 1986. The system which has been predominantly used, and is now the electoral law once more, is that of the second ballot. Basically the principle employed here is that no matter how many candidates may be nominated for a single seat the successful one must have a majority over all the other candidates combined.[38] This method has been tried in many European countries but was abandoned everywhere except in France.

Election is by absolute majority in two ballots within a single member constituency. To be elected in the first ballot, a candidate must obtain an absolute majority and at least one quarter of the valid votes cast by registered electors. In the second ballot, which takes place one week later, a relative majority is sufficient. Only candidates polling at least 10% of the valid votes cast in the first ballot may take part in the second one. Should, however, only one candidate fulfil this condition, then the candidate with the second highest number of votes is admitted to the second ballot. If no candidate fulfils the conditions, then the second ballot takes place between the two candidates polling the most votes in the first round.[39]

The French system gives rise to the possibility and, indeed, the necessity, of tactical voting in the second round.

Parties may enter into agreements that they will support the highest among them in the first round as their joint candidate in the second or they may work out some other more elaborate carve-up in order to secure some equity in the seats to be won. The Union de la Gauche between the Socialists and the Communists, which brought Mitterrand to power in 1981, is an example of such tactics and can be regarded as analogous to lower preference voting within STV.

## The List System

Of the countries remaining in the European Community, all use the list system and they can be analysed separately in terms of voter choice amongst the candidates on the list and the method of allocating seats.

As regards voter choice in Italy, the voter votes for a list and may, but need not, alter the numbering of the candidates.

Likewise in Belgium, the voter may alter the list. But in the Netherlands, as in Finland, the voter numbers one of the candidates within a party list. Any candidate whose personal votes exceed the quota is elected and any surplus votes are transferred to other candidates in the order in which they stand in the party list. In Denmark the voter also has a choice between voting a party list as it stands and marking one candidate on it.

The Danish system is complicated because in each polling district the candidate nominated for that district appears first on that list. A candidate receives two types of votes i.e. all the personal votes plus the list votes in the district where they head the list. Candidates with the most votes fill the seats allocated to their party. As a further complication, a party may place all its candidates in a constituency on an equal footing, in which case their election depends solely on personal votes.

As may be expected, however, the number of voters exercising a personal choice within a predetermined list is very small so the parties effectively determine the order in which the candidates are chosen. Both Sweden and Austria allow the voter to cross out names on a list but this has effect only if done by more than half of the party's supporters, which in practice rarely happens.[40] Where the elector cannot vote without marking an individual candidate, as in the Netherlands (and also in Finland and Switzerland), differences in personal support for candidates come out strongly.[40] For the purpose of completeness it should be noted that the Norwegians simply vote for a party list.

In summary, it can be concluded that the list system usually provides an elector with the theoretical right to alter the order in which candidates are to be elected – it being understood, of course, that candidates are elected in descending order as they appear on the list. Denmark and the Netherlands provide for individual choice (as do Finland and Switzerland) but whatever the degree of personal choice the vote is essentially locked into a party and cannot escape unlike the STV system where cross party voting is endemic.

The reason is, of course, that the STV system is not based on parties but on individuals and the list system is not based on individuals but on parties.

## Vote Counting Methods

The European Parliament published a helpful research paper in 1988 entitled 'Electoral Laws of Parliaments of the Member States of the European Communities' from which the following material is drawn.

Vote counting methods can be divided into two main types: the quota method and the largest average method. The basic difference between them is not so much the method of calculation as in the result. In their commonest forms, quota methods do not usually result in the allocation of all the seats and those left over have to be allocated by means of another method of calculation. Divisor methods, on the other hand, invariably permit the allocation of all seats.

The quota method, as we in Ireland know, is based on the principle that a seat is allocated for a given number of votes and is obtained by dividing the valid number of votes cast by the number of seats to be allocated or that number plus one, two or three etc. The commonest, as in Ireland, is the number of seats plus one.

In the largest average method, the number of votes obtained by the parties is divided by a series of numbers and the seats are allocated according to the size of the resulting quotients. The commonest system is the d'Hondt method whereby the votes are divided by a series: 1-2-3-4

Belgium uses the d'Hondt method. Where all the seats cannot be distributed directly in the constituency, the remainder is distributed at province level among all groups of lists which have obtained at least 66% of the elector divisor in a constituency. Seats are usually allocated to candidates on the lists according to the order in which they are entered.

In Italy, on the other hand, the number of votes cast is divided by the number of seats plus two and each list is allocated as many seats as it has complete quotas. Within the lists, seats are awarded on the basis of the preference votes, although these will probably not distort the original order. Seats which are not filled in the constituencies are distributed proportionally at national level but only to parties polling at least 300,000 votes in the whole country.

The Netherlands uses a quota system by calculating a national quota and seats not allocated by this method are distributed by the rule of the largest average. Within the lists the seats are then subdivided to individuals using quotas yet again.

In Denmark, the seats are shared among the parties in proportion to their totals and personal votes using a modification of the d'Hondt rule. Forty supplementary seats are allocated to make the results as proportional as possible.

This system is also used in Sweden where voting takes place on regional lists. Stockholm, for example, is a region with its own lists. The forty supplementary seats are allocated to the parties that have either won seats in a region or secured more than 4% of the national vote. The net result is that parliamentary representation is proportional to a party's national vote.

## Recommendations

This analysis could be extended but it would become too complex in terms of detail. Suffice it to say that the Continental norm is a list system in which parties receive a share of the seats proportional to their vote and in which candidates are elected in the order of preference as determined by the parties and not by the electors. This has an inevitable consequence for both the quality of the parliamentary members and the style of parliamentary politics, consequences from which we might benefit.

That is another issue for another day. For the moment it remains to be recommended that our constitution should specify PR as the electoral system without indicating which form of PR is to be used and leaving it to the Oireachtas to decide on the system to be employed, as under the 1922 Constitution. That would give us the flexibility to, perhaps, use the German system for the Dáil, STV for the Senate and the list system for the European Elections.

If the Senate were to be genuinely based on social and economic interests other than parties then the STV system would be an appropriate method of election. Indeed, it would be ideal.

As for the European Parliament elections, STV has turned out to be an absurd method of election for the simple reason that the constituencies are too big. The problem will become accentuated as the number of Irish MEPs falls due to future enlargement of the Community.

I proposed, as Party Secretary, in 1974 that the Bill providing for direct elections to the European Parliament, which first took place in 1979, should stipulate a national list system.

Unfortunately, the responsible Minister, Jimmy Tully of my own party, and other Ministers generally, were simply not interested. A great opportunity was lost to familiarize the electorate with the workings of the list system and, incidentally, to return members better attuned to the style of the European Parliament.

It is not too late to remedy that lamentable mistake. It can be done by legislation and does not require a referendum. It is an intriguing thought for those bent on reform. It would be beneficial in its own right and might start the process of more fundamental reform.

## Conclusion

The electoral system is the spine of the political system. It determines the quality of the parliamentarians elected to represent the nation and, in turn, the quality of the government they elect to manage our collective affairs as a people.

It is deeply regrettable, and profoundly disquieting, that it has not been subjected to forensic examination on the basis of what is best for a parliamentary democracy. It should be.

Electoral reform suffers from the handicap that it is neither a popular nor a populist subject for public debate and will prove difficult to move it up the political agenda. But those concerned for the future of their country should try to put it at the head of the constitutional reform agenda. Failing to reform the electoral system may otherwise prove fatal for politics itself.

# Chapter Four

## A Word to the Wise

*A Submission to the Parliamentary Labour Party, 2007*

# 4. A Word to the Wise

## Background

The following paper was drafted for the Parliamentary Labour Party as a contribution to its submission to the Constituencies Commission in 2007. The material was not employed, presumably because it showed the STV system had, perversely, begun to favour the party, as in the 2007 election.

The key point made was that the number of five-seaters determines the proportionality of STV as a whole.

Throughout the submission STV is equated with Proportional Representation and used inter-changeably with PR. This is not, of course, true. STV is not a form of PR but establishing that truth was a battle for another time and place.

## Section One: General Context

### Origins of the Commission

The original purpose of the Constituency Commission was to ensure that the system of proportional representation (PR), as introduced into the constitution of Saorstát

Éireann and retained in Bunreacht na h-Éireann (Article 16.2.5) would be allowed to operate as intended. The article states that in respect of the National Parliament "The members shall be elected on the system of proportional representation by means of the single transferable vote".

While there are many forms of PR to be considered, their common underlying purpose is to ensure that in a general election political parties should secure seats in parliament in proportion to their share of the national vote.

The people of Ireland, who are the enactors of the constitution, have on four occasions endorsed and upheld PR as the electoral system of their choice. On the last two occasions when the matter was put to them for resolution in referenda called by Fianna Fáil governments they expressly chose to retain STV over the British "first past the post" system.

The people's refusal to jettison PR in 1968 provoked a revision of the constituencies a year later, which immediately drew sustained criticism from the Labour Party on the grounds that having failed to ditch PR in a referendum the Fianna Fáil government was intent on subverting the system by reducing its proportionality effect.

## Number of Constituencies

This deliberate dilution of the proportionality of STV was to be achieved not only by substantially increasing the number of three seat constituencies and drastically reducing the number of five seaters but also by concentrating the three seaters in regions where the Fianna Fáil vote was strongest and four seaters in regions where it was weakest.

A comparison of the distribution of constituency sizes between the 1961 and 1969 revisions clearly demonstrates that the purpose of the latter revision was to dilute the proportionality effect of STV, thereby giving Fianna Fáil a larger bonus of seats over votes than had been the norm.

| Table One Size of Constituencies | | | | |
|---|---|---|---|---|
| Year of Revision | 3 Seats | 4 Seats | 5 Seats | Total |
| 1961 | 17 | 12 | 9 | 38 |
| 1969 | 26 | 14 | 2 | 42 |

The most significant effect of this change in the distribution of constituency sizes was the increase in the number of three seaters from seventeen to twenty-six and the corresponding reduction in the number of five seaters from nine to two. It is accepted by political scientists that proportionality and constituency size are inversely correlated, and that the larger the size of constituencies the greater the proportionality of the system as a whole. It is self evident from these analytical insights that the 1969 revision was consciously intended to use these features of STV for partisan purposes.

The impact on the proportionality of the system as a whole was profound and can be gauged from the number of TDs elected per size of constituency as set out here in Table Two.

| Table Two Number of TDs per size of Constituency | | | | |
|---|---|---|---|---|
| Year of Revision | 3 Seats | 4 Seats | 5 Seats | Total |
| 1961 | 51 | 48 | 45 | 144 |
| 1969 | 78 | 56 | 10 | 144 |

The percentage of TDs elected per size of constituency is even more revealing as means of demonstrating the political intent behind the constituency revision. As the Table Three below proves, the net effect was a drastic alteration in the distribution of deputies by size of constituency in favour of the smallest possible constituency and to the detriment of the largest permissible under legislation.

| Table Three % TDs elected per size of Constituency | | | | |
|---|---|---|---|---|
| Year of Revision | 3 Seats | 4 Seats | 5 Seats | Total |
| 1961 | 35.4% | 33.3% | 31.3% | 100% |
| 1969 | 54.2% | 38.9% | 6.9% | 100% |

The above table illustrates the profound shift in the make-up of the Dáil. Whereas the number of members elected from each size of constituency had been roughly equal the situation had been changed to one where over half the members were elected in three seaters, with only 7% coming from five seaters. The constituency system was effectively reduced to that of three and four seaters, with the very minimum of five seaters being retained for the sake of appearances. The full implications of this radical rearrangement of constituencies is examined in more depth in the following section but the paragraphs below summarise the repercussions in terms of the events which led to the formation of the Constituency Commission.

## Political Repercussions of the 1969 Electoral Act

The immediate effect on the proportionality of the system can be seen from Table Four in which the percentages of votes won in the 1965 and 1969 general elections are each compared with the percentages of Dáil seats gained by the three main parties.

The difference between the two percentages is then expressed as either a bonus or a deficit. In a truly proportional system the two percentages would, of course, be identical. As the table below demonstrates the difference between seats and votes increased by more than a factor of three in the case of the Fianna Fáil party. This is hardly surprising as that is precisely what the constituency revision was intended to achieve in the 1969 general election.

| Table Four |||
|---|---|---|
| Difference in percentage votes and seats |||
| Election 1965 |||
| | Votes | Seats | Difference |
|---|---|---|---|
| Fianna Fáil | 47.8% | 50.0% | + 2.2% |
| Fine Gael | 33.0% | 32.6% | - 0.8% |
| Labour | 15.4% | 14.6% | 0.8% |

| Table Four (2) |||
|---|---|---|
| Election 1969 |||
| | Votes | Seats | Difference |
|---|---|---|---|
| Fianna Fáil | 44.6% | 51.4% | + 6.8% |
| Fine Gael | 33.3% | 34.7% | + 1.4% |
| Labour | 16.6% | 12.5% | 4.1% |

This disparity between the percentage of votes won nationally and seats gained in the Dáil led to retaliation on the part of the Fine Gael and Labour Party government which was elected in 1973 on foot of a pre-election voting pact. The constituencies were revised in 1974 as follows:

| Table Five ||||
|---|---|---|---|
| Constituencies per number of TDs ||||
| Year of Revision | 3 Seats | 4 Seats | 5 Seats | Total |
|---|---|---|---|---|
| 1969 | 26 | 14 | 2 | 42 |
| 1974 | 26 | 10 | 6 | 42 |

At first sight, the two schemes do not appear to be significantly different, given that the number of three seaters was the same at twenty-six each. But this mathematical identity marked a major shift in the regional location of the three seaters from west of the Shannon to the Dublin area. Despite this switch in regional concentration, and notwithstanding the increase in the number of five seaters, the subsequent general election in 1977 again gave rise to a disproportionate allocation of seats between the three main parties.

### The Constituencies Commission

The upshot of this decade of controversy over the electoral system was that the parties effectively called a truce on trying to bias the mechanics of the system in favour of whosoever was in power. It was agreed on the basis of a broad consensus that the periodic revision of the constituencies should be depoliticised and made the responsibility of an independent commission.

It is immediately evident from this brief history of the origins of the Constituencies Commission that its raison d'etre is to protect the integrity of the STV system as a form of proportional representation from political bias or interference and, additionally, to ensure that the electoral system functions as intended by Article 16.2.5 of the constitution.

It follows that if the members of Dáil Éireann are to be "elected on the system of proportional representation" then the fundamental requirement is to protect and give effect to the proportionality of the system as a whole and that this feature of the system must be given precedence over what can only be regarded as secondary characteristics or mechanical concerns, such as county boundaries, continuity in relation to the arrangements of constituencies or regard for significant physical features.

From a reading of the Commission Report 2004 (Pr 1554) this does not appear to have been the case. The concluding paragraph of Section 3.4 page 12 is instructive in this regard when it states that:

"Overall, we did not set out with a preconceived view as to the number and location of the different sizes of constituency but, in complying with the constitutional requirements and our terms of reference we endeavoured to suit the constituency size to the population and particular circumstances of each locality."

This is precisely the wrong point of departure. The Commission should have had a preconceived view as to the number of the different sizes of constituency. Contrary to the position it adopted, it should be guided by the fundamental requirement of ensuring a close approximation between votes cast and the seats won so that proportional representation is achieved in practice. This objective requires, in turn, that the appropriate balance between the different sizes of constituency should be determined *a priori* rather than emerging as the consequence of suiting "the constituency size to the population and particular circumstances of each locality".

As Table Four above demonstrated, the number and

location of the different sizes of constituency have the most serious implications for the size of the parties in Dáil Éireann and can, quite literally, determine who goes into government and who is condemned to opposition. For this reason, the substantive argument being presented here is that the Commission must, above all, have due regard to the number of the different sizes of constituency if STV is to behave as a system of proportional representation.

In effect, the Commission's choice of the number of the different sizes of constituencies and their location has profound political implications.

In order to reinforce this point the following section analyses the factors which determine the proportionality of STV and draws on academic studies as appropriate.

v

## Section Two: Factors affecting the proportionality of STV

### The Size of Constituencies

The STV system is differentiated from other forms of PR in two ways. Under STV the voter chooses between individual candidates whereas in most other PR systems the choice is between parties or lists of candidates submitted by the parties (Germany has a hybrid system of individual candidates and parties).

Secondly, STV is distinguished by a large number

of small constituencies whereas under list systems the opposite is true and in extreme cases the whole country acts as a single constituency.

It has long been accepted by psephologists that size of constituencies – "district magnitude" as it is called in the United States – is a variable affecting proportionality (O'Leary, 1979, 108). This proposition was expressed in 1945 by Hogan (Hogan, 1945, 13) as follows:

> "The decisive point in PR is the size of the constituencies, the larger the constituency, that is, the greater the number of members which it elects, the more closely will the result approximate to proportionality. On the other hand, the smaller the constituency, that is, the fewer the number of members which it returns, the more radical will be the departure from proportionality".

This proposition is a mathematical truism since the larger the constituency the smaller the quota – they are inversely related – and the greater the prospect of voter preferences being reflected in the number of seats won by the respective parties.

## Trends in Constituency sizes

That being so, it might have been expected that the number of deputies elected in five seat constituencies would predominate and that recourse to three and four seaters would be regarded as a departure from the norm, justified perhaps by the necessity to accommodate to significant physical features in special circumstances. That, of course, is not the case. The reverse has been happening and the five-seat constituency is becoming the exception rather than the rule, as Table Six demonstrates.

| Table Six: Five Seat Constituencies | | | |
|---|---|---|---|
| Year | No. of constituents | No. of TDs | % of Dáil |
| 1980 | 15 | 75 | 45% |
| 1990 | 14 | 70 | 42% |
| 2003 | 12 | 60 | 36% |

The corollary, of course, is that the number of three seaters has been increasing, thereby automatically diluting the proportionality effect of the system as a whole.

| Table Seven: Three Seat Constituencies | | | |
|---|---|---|---|
| Year | No. of constituents | No. of TDs | % of Dáil |
| 1990 | 12 | 36 | 22% |
| 1998 | 16 | 48 | 29% |
| 2003 | 18 | 54 | 33% |

## Other Factors

It has to be said, of course, that other factors also influence the proportionality of the general election results. All other things being equal, the outcome can be affected by a pre-election pact between parties to transfer votes between them; the 1969 and 1973 general elections being the classic example of this phenomenon (see Knight and Baxter-Moore, 1973). In addition, the number of parties contesting the election can have a major influence on the proportionality of the outcome. Likewise, the impact of independents. But all that having been said, it can be taken as a sound rule of thumb that electoral systems have significant political implications (see Douglas Rae, The Political Consequences of Electoral Laws, 1971). This is particularly true of the prevalence of three and four seat constituencies in the STV system.

## Index of Proportionality

One measure of the proportionality of any system of PR is what O'Leary calls "the index of proportionality". The index is derived by dividing the percentage of seats won by the percentage of votes won, full proportionality being represented by the figure 100. Alternatively, it can be also determined by dividing the number of seats won by the number of seats that would have been won in proportion to votes. O'Leary used the index to measure the proportionality of Irish elections between 1923 and 1977 (O'Leary, 1979, pps 100 – 110).

Table Eight below calculates the index since the February 1982 general election for each of the three main political parties.

| Table Eight: Index of Proportionality | | | |
|---|---|---|---|
| Election | Fianna Fáil | Fine Gael | Labour |
| 1982 (Feb) | 103 | 102 | 99 |
| 1982 (Nov) | 103 | 108 | 102 |
| 1987 | 107 | 111 | 113 |
| 1989 | 105 | 113 | 96 |
| 1992 | 105 | 111 | 104 |
| 1997 | 120 | 117 | 98 |
| 2002 | 118 | 83 | 111 |
| 2007 | 112 | 112 | 119 |

## Bonus Seats for Fianna Fáil

It is evident that there has been a pronounced upward shift in the index in favour of Fianna Fáil over the past three elections. Whereas the index averaged 104 during the decade 1982–92 it rose to an average of 117 over the most recent decade 1997–2007. It follows that the number of bonus seats won by Fianna Fáil has risen substantially in each of the past three general elections, as Table Nine proves.

| Table Nine: Bonus Seats for Fianna Fáil | | | |
|---|---|---|---|
| | Proportionate Seats | Actual Seats | Bonus Won Seats |
| 1982 | 79 | 81 | 2 |
| 1987 | 73 | 81 | 8 |
| 1989 | 73 | 77 | 4 |
| 1992 | 65 | 68 | 3 |
| 1997 | 65 | 77 | 12 |
| 2002 | 69 | 81 | 12 |
| 2007 | 69 | 77 | 8 |

*The return of the outgoing Ceann Comhairle is excluded where applicable from the number of seats won*

## The Impact of Constituency Size

The bonus seats arose from the predominance of three and four seaters in the system. As was argued above, three seaters allow a large party like Fianna Fáil to maximise the effectiveness of its vote where it is electorally strongest and to minimise the effectiveness of its opponent votes in constituencies where it is at its weakest. This was the strategy behind the Fianna Fáil revision in 1969. It is remarkable that this is how the current location of different constituency sizes worked out in practice in the 2007 election.

| Table Ten: Fianna Fáil Bonus Seats 2007 General Election ||||||| 
| Constit. Size | Votes % votes | Seats Won % seats | Entitle-ment | Actual Seats Won | Bonus Deficit | Propor-tionality Index |
|---|---|---|---|---|---|---|
| 3 seats | 43.9% | 51.9% | 23 | 28 | 5 | 118 |
| 4 seats | 39.8% | 46.4% | 20 | 24 | 4 | 117 |
| 5 seats | 41.9% | 41.8% | 25 | 24 | -1 | 100 |

While the above table contains rounded up figures for the number of seats proportionate to the votes won the conclusions to be drawn are unambiguous. The three seat constituencies confer the biggest bonus of seats on Fianna Fáil and have a Proportionality Index of 118. The four seaters, despite recording the lowest percentage of votes for Fianna Fáil, also confer a significant bonus of seats on that party and have a Proportionality Index of 117. It is only the five seat constituencies that correlate votes and seats won.

This bears out the point made throughout this submission that a large number of three and four seat constituencies will distort the proportionality of the system as a whole and that the surest guarantee of a high degree of proportionality is the presence of a large number of five seat constituencies.

## Conclusion

The Constituency Commission should start with a decision on the configuration of constituency sizes which it believes would best guarantee a reasonable degree of proportionality between the votes cast for the parties and the seats won by them. By way of illustration, the following configuration would meet the objective implicit in Article 16.2.5 of the Constitution:

> Thirteen 3-Seaters returning 23% of the TDs.
> Twelve 4-Seaters returning 29% of the TDs.
> Sixteen 5-Seaters returning 48% of the TDs.

The number of TDs would under this formula be increased to 167.

The current configuration of constituency sizes frustrates the intent of the constitution and the will of the people who enacted and protected its provisions. Any further increase in the number of either three or four seaters would only serve to add to the current distortion in the translation of votes into seats. It must be resisted.

# Chapter Five

## In the Heat of Battle

*Article for "The Sunday Independent," February 1982*

## 5. In the Heat of Battle

### Alternative Voting Systems

There's no question about it and nobody needs an opinion poll to verify it. The public don't want another election. The demand is for a strong government, a stable government, a national government. It all boils down to the same thing. The people want a majority government which will last. The problem is that the election results didn't turn out that way. Neither side, for the second time in seven months, won either an absolute majority of the votes or of the seats in Dáil Éireann.

In one sense we can't complain. Our electoral system is performing in exactly the way it was intended. It is producing a pretty good correlation between the votes cast for each party nationally and seats won in the Dáil. Since nobody gained an overall majority of the votes nobody has gained an overall majority of the seats. So we have a hung Dáil. Seven deputies hold the key to power; a minor party of three and a disparate group of four independents.

There's nothing new about this. Since Fianna Fáil came to power in 1932 there have been seventeen elections, including this one. In only seven have Fianna Fáil won an absolute majority of seats. That's contrary to what most people think, perceiving Fianna Fáil as a "natural majority" party. They are not. They are easily the largest party, and have consistently been that, but one must distinguish between being the biggest and being a majority. They are not synonymous.

Out of the nine elections in which Fianna Fáil were returned as a minority party they actually formed a Government on no less than five occasions. In these cases they relied on a variety of support: Labour twice and independents the rest of the time. Four times, and four times only, were they unable to turn their minority of seats into a Government with outside help. And, of course, we still don't know what's going to happen on the 9th March.

The Fianna Fáil track record is simple. Seven outright wins as a majority, five times in government even though a minority party, four spells in opposition and one as yet undecided. So what's wrong this time? There are a couple of factors which have made these last seven months unique. Firstly, this is the first time when an election held within a year of a previous one has failed to produce a decisive result. The precedents are 1927, 1933, 1938 and 1944. We have never had two successive indecisive results before. And people don't like it.

Secondly, these last two general elections are the only ones so far fought on constituencies not arranged by the politicians themselves. The present boundaries were drawn up independently by an impartial Commission and this has had the effect of filtering out what might be called, the "gerrymander factor". In many ways this is the key to the "hung Dáil" situation and is best explained by going back to Fianna Fáil's seven majority governments. Odd as it may seem they only won a majority of votes nationally on two of those occasions. On the other five, they got a "bonus" of seats, which ensured a majority in Dáil Éireann, simply by being the largest party, as well as being the party which had actually drawn up the constituency boundaries. That 'bonus' was, at times, as high as 6.5% and meant that Fianna Fáil got 6.5% more of the Dáil seats than their votes strictly entitled them to. In practical terms it meant they got an extra six to nine seats, enough to take them over the top.

But the independent commission has weakened the "bonus" factor to the extent that I estimate Fianna Fáil must in future win 48.5% of the votes in order to be certain of winning over 50% of the seats. At present, they are 1.25% short of that critical figure. Just how difficult it would be to reach that target can be gauged from the following chilling statistic: in seventeen outings they have only exceeded it on three occasions. From now on a majority Fianna Fáil Government will be the exception rather than the rule. The same is equally true of any Fine Gael/Labour Coalition.

The prospects are for a continuous series of minority governments, each dependent on small parties and independents - and each with a future as uncertain as an April day. If we want stable majority Government made up of one or more major parties then we must do one of two things. We either change the present alignment of the major parties in the Dáil or we change the system of voting to produce majority Government out of minority parties. The most stable government theoretically possible at present is a Fianna Fáil/Fine Gael Coalition. It would have a majority of 144 seats. It would be something like the Grand coalitions in Germany and Austria which both worked well in terms of the problems they set out to solve.

The next most stable government would be a Fianna Fáil/Labour Coalition or a Fianna Fáil minority government supported by Labour, as happened in 1932 and 1937. It would have a majority of 26. Ironically, this year is the fiftieth anniversary of Labour bringing Fianna Fáil to power for the first time in 1932. There is no other stable government in sight bar a Fianna Fáil/Left Alliance, which is unlikely.

All of the above, while theoretically possible, are not yet within the gambit of political practicalities. That being the case, we had better steel ourselves for a succession of short-lived minority governments. That will have the undoubted effect of many people questioning an electoral system which produces such instability. But what could we put in place of our system of proportional representation?

Well for a start, the British 'first past the post' system has been twice rejected by way of referendum. And they may get rid of it anyway in the near future. That's out. There was an interesting variation on the British system put forward in the last PR referendum, the so-called Norton Amendment. This was the Australian method of electing deputies from single member constituencies but using the simple transferable vote as at present. Without question this would produce a huge Fianna Fáil majorities, giving them well over one hundred seats on present party strengths. Many people rightly felt this would be too high a price to pay for stability.

There are two other single member constituency systems in use: France and Germany. In France voters go to the polls and simply put an "X" opposite the candidate of their choice, as in Britain. Candidates who win more than 50% of the votes are elected. If, as is more likely, nobody wins a majority, then a play off is held a week later between the two candidates who got the most votes in the first round. This system is consciously designed to produce majority governments. It does; but at the expense of fairness to the minority parties.

The German system seems more attractive. Here half the Bundestag is elected in single member constituencies, as in Britain. But the other half is elected from party lists. In addition to the seats won in the constituencies each party is allocated a certain number of seats from their lists so that they finish up with the same percentage of seats in the Bundestag as their national percentage of the votes. If you get 50% of the votes you get 50% of the seats. In this way they remove the distorting effect of the British system. Neat and logical, typically German.

Except not quite. A party must get more than 4% of the national vote before it can be represented in Parliament.

On that basis, Sinn Féin the Workers Party would not have any seats at all in this Dáil.

The system is deliberately designed to keep out the minor parties, such as, in Germany, the communist parties. This results in the larger parties always getting a bonus of additional seats when they share out those seats which otherwise would have gone to splinter groups. If the German system were in use here the result of this month's election would have been: Fianna Fáil 84, Fine Gael 66 and Labour 16. That would have given a majority to Fianna Fáil, albeit a small one. But these days a majority is a majority.

Or we could go for the Swedish model, which would give the same overall result as the German system, but through a different route. In Sweden voters vote in multi-member constituencies much bigger than in Ireland but they vote for the party of their choice, not the candidate. This is the 'list system'.

Interestingly, it was used in all the member states for the 1979 European Parliament Elections, with the exception of the UK and Ireland. Its popularity is obviously increasing and inevitably it will be used here when a uniform voting system is employed in some future Euro-elections.

In our present circumstances the list system has two great attractions. If the 4% hurdle is invoked then the eventual result will nearly always produce a majority Government. But it will also produce a Government elected on the issues and not on the personalities of the local T.D.s.

All the evidence is that Irish voters overwhelmingly vote on the basis of personal popularity. The personality of the candidates predominates, not their policies. The multi-member constituency inevitably brings that about. The most intense competition now is not between parties but within parties. The bitterest rivals are candidates standing on the same ticket. Our memories are fresh. The examples are there. As Albert Reynolds said on election night: we had forty-one General Elections in forty-one constituencies. That was not the way it was supposed to be. In fact, the party system as we know it is breaking down under the stress of competition between party colleagues. It is time we gave the electoral system a long cool examination.

Don't forget we never chose the present voting system for ourselves. It was given to us by the British. The only other places to use it are Malta and Tasmania. Obviously, it is not universally popular. Is it time to consciously choose an alternative? Circumstances are dictating that the answer is "Yes".

# References

# References

## Chapter 3: Sailing Under False Colours

01. Bogdanor, Vernon: *What is Proportional Representation*, Oxford, 1984, p.77

02. Meredith, James Creed: *Proportional Representation in Practice*, Dublin 1913

03. Commons, John R: *Proportional Representation*, London 1907

04. Commons, John R: As above, p.15

05. Royal Commission on Electoral Systems

06. Humphreys, John J: *Proportional Representation*, London 1911, p.196

07. Humphreys. John J: As above, p.198

08. Electoral Reform Society: *The Case for the Single Transferrable Vote*, London 1982, p.20

09. Hoag and Hallett: *Proportional Representation*, New York 1926, Appendix 1

10. Maude and Szemery: *Why Electoral Change?* London 1982

11. Meredith, James Creed: As above, p.100

12. Humphreys, John J: *Proportional Representation*, London 1911, p.197

13. Hain and Hodgson: *Proportional Misrepresentation?*, Nottingham 1982, p.12

14. Maude and Szemery : *Why Electoral Change?*, London 1982, p.26

15. Hoag and Hallett: *Proportional Representation*, New York 1926, Appendix 1

16. O'Leary, Cornelius: *Irish Elections* 1918-1977, Dublin 1978, p.5

17. O'Leary, Cornelius: As above, p.6

18. Hansard: *Irish Affairs* 1912, Vol 2, Cols 2454/57

19. Hansard, Col Greigor MP : As above, Col 2461

20. Hansard: Newman MP : *Irish Affairs* 1912, Vol 3, Col 2461

21. Hansard: As above, 1912, Vol 43, Col 960

22. Hansard: As above, 1912, Vol 43, Col 1096

23. Hoag and Hulles: As above, p.253

24. Lakeman, Enid: *Power to Elect*, London, 1982, p.86

25. O'Leary, Cornelius: *The Irish Republic and its Experiment with Proportional Representation*, Notre Dame, 1962, p4

26. O'Leary, Cornelius: *Irish Elections*, 1918-1977, Dublin, 1979, p4

27. Mac Ardle, Dorothy: *The Irish Republic*, London, 1937, p.325-526

28. O'Sullivan, Donal: *The Irish Free State and Its Senate*, London, 1940, p.76

29. Farrell, Brian: *The Drafting of the Irish Free State Constitution*, Irish Jurist, New Series 1970, Vol 5, p131

30. Farrell, Brian: *The Drafting of the Irish Free State Constitution*, Irish Jurist, New Series 1970, Vol 5, p.127

31. O'Leary, Cornelius : *Irish Elections*, 1961, p.12

32. O'Leary, Cornelius : As above, 1979, p.15

33. O'Leary, Cornelius: As above, 1979, p.14

34. O'Leary, Cornelius: As above, 1961, p.1

35. Meredith, James Creed: *Proportional Representation in Practice*, Dublin 1913, p.82

36. This was the situation in 1987. As of 2010 some twenty-two of the twenty-seven Member States of the European Union used the list system.

37. Lakeman Enid: *How Democracies Vote*, London 1986, p.208-213

38. Lakeman Enid: As above, p.61

39. European Parliament: Electoral Laws of Parliaments of Member States of the European Communities, p.80

40. Lakeman Enid: 1976, as above, p.105-106

41. Lakeman Enid: 1976, as above, p.107

## Chapter 4. A Word to the Wise

O'Leary, Cornelius

Hogan, Patrick

Knight and Baxter-Moore, Douglas, Ray, *The Political Consequences of Electoral Laws*, 1971

www.scathanpress.com

www.ingramcontent.com/pod-product-compliance
Lightning Source LLC
Chambersburg PA
CBHW032042290426
44110CB00012B/914